THE KING
IN ORANGE

"Against a humorous and informed survey of the American political landscape, Greer analyzes the 2016 U.S. presidential election through the lens of magic. Taking his cue from Ioan P. Couliano's masterpiece *Eros and Magic in the Renaissance,* Greer shows the power of symbols in forming popular opinion and political action and with it the competing and combating views of magic of the two principal parties: the magic of the privileged versus pragmatic positivism and where they meet in the Faustian dream of perpetual progress. An essential book for anyone seeking to understand the direction in which 'cancel culture,' the industrial world, and its formerly liberal democracies are heading."

MARK STAVISH, AUTHOR OF *EGREGORES*

"John Michael Greer is one of the true original minds on the scene in these rather dire days of the wobbling American experiment. His books hack through the precooked ideology of our so-called thinking classes to present always-fresh connections between events on the ground and the deep mysteries of our being here in the first place, especially the issues of good and evil, which so befog us today."

JAMES HOWARD KUNSTLER, AUTHOR OF *THE LONG EMERGENCY*

THE KING IN ORANGE

THE MAGICAL AND OCCULT ROOTS OF POLITICAL POWER

JOHN MICHAEL GREER

Inner Traditions
Rochester, Vermont

Inner Traditions
One Park Street
Rochester, Vermont 05767
www.InnerTraditions.com

Text stock is SFI certified

Cataloging-in-Publication Data for this title is available from the Library of Congress

ISBN 978-1-64411-258-8 (print)
ISBN 978-1-64411-259-5 (ebook)

Printed and bound in the United States by Lake Book Manufacturing, Inc.
The text stock is SFI certified. The Sustainable Forestry Initiative® program
promotes sustainable forest management.

10   9   8   7   6   5   4   3   2   1

Text design and layout by Priscilla H. Baker
This book was typeset in Garamond Premier Pro with Mackay, Majesty, and
Trenda used as display typefaces

To send correspondence to the author of this book, mail a first-class letter to the
author c/o Inner Traditions • Bear & Company, One Park Street, Rochester, VT
05767, and we will forward the communication, or contact the author directly at
www.ecosophia.net.

Contents

✸

Along the shore the cloud waves break,
The two suns sink beneath the lake,
The shadows lengthen
*   In Carcosa.*

Strange is the night where black stars rise,
And strange moons circle through the skies,
But stranger still is
*   Lost Carcosa.*

Songs that the Hyades shall sing,
Where flap the tatters of the King,
Must die unheard in
*   Dim Carcosa.*

Song of my soul, my song is dead,
Die thou unsung, as tears unshed
Shall dry and die in
*   Lost Carcosa.*

"CASSILDA'S SONG"
IN *THE KING IN YELLOW*

INTRODUCTION

Under Some Kind of Magic Spell

Ne raillons pas les fous; leur folie dure plus longtemps que la nôtre. . . . Voilà toute la difference. (Don't make fun of madmen. Their madness lasts longer than ours. . . . That's the only difference.)

FROM "THE REPAIRER OF REPUTATIONS"
IN *THE KING IN YELLOW*

We like to think, most of us, that we live in a world that makes rational sense. The dominant narratives of the industrial world portray the universe as a vast machine governed by rigid deterministic laws, in which everything that will ever happen could be known in advance, if only we could just gather enough data. Our political expectations are much the same: we elect candidates because they claim to be able to make the machinery of representative democracy do what we want it to do, and the mere fact that things never quite manage to work that way never seems to shake the conviction that they will, or at least that they should.

It's all a pretense, and we know it. The reason we can be sure it's a pretense is that when some part of the world misbehaves in a way that won't allow the fantasy to be maintained, a great many of us respond with rage. We aren't baffled or intrigued or stunned; we're furious that the universe has seen fit to break the rules *again*—and of course it's that "again," stated or unstated, that gives away the game. We know at some level that the rules in question are simply a set of narratives in the heads of some not very bright social primates on the third lump of rock from a midsized star nowhere in particular in a very big universe. Most of us cling to the narratives anyway, since the alternative is to let go and fall free into a wider and stranger world, where we can't count on being able to predict or control anything.

Sometimes, though, the pretense becomes very, very hard to maintain. In case you haven't noticed, we're living in one of those times. It's a source of fascination and wry amusement to me that the event that plunged us into a realm of paradox, tore open the familiar world of half-truths and comfortable evasions, and sent a great many of us spinning off into the void, wasn't any of the grandiose cataclysms or cosmic leaps of consciousness so luridly portrayed by the last three or four generations of would-be prophets. It wasn't the arrival of the space brothers or the Second Coming of Christ or the end of the thirteenth baktun of the Mayan calendar. No, it was the election of an elderly reality-television star, wrestling promoter, and real estate mogul named Donald Trump to the presidency of the United States of America.

Just when we crossed over the border into nonordinary reality is an interesting question, and it's one I'm far from sure I can answer exactly. Well over a year before the 2016 election, certainly, I noticed that something very strange was happening out there in the twilight realms of the American imagination, something that the corporate media weren't covering and pundits and politicians seemed to be going out of their way to ignore. By the new year I was certain that politics as usual were about to be chucked out the window, and less than a month later—on January 20, 2016, to be precise—I posted an essay to the blog I wrote in those days, *The Archdruid Report,* titled "Donald Trump and the Politics of Resentment." In it I talked about some of the reasons that the bipartisan political consensus in the United States was coming apart at the seams and predicted that Trump would win the election.

In the months that followed I expanded on that prediction, watched in bemusement as Trump's campaign turned nimble and clever while Clinton's stumbled from one self-inflicted disaster to another, and caught my first glimpses of deeper and stranger forces at work under the pretense of business as usual. I started hearing about "the chans," Pepe the frog, a forgotten Europop song titled "Shadilay," and an ancient Egyptian god named Kek. In my blog posts I tried to sketch out a first tentative outline of the landscape of politics and consciousness that was coming into view as Trump's campaign shrugged off the sustained attacks of the entire U.S. political and corporate establishment and pulled off a victory that most respectable thinkers at the time considered utterly impossible.

It was the aftermath, however, that made it clear just how far we'd strayed into the absolute elsewhere. Just after the election, I thought that the tantrums being thrown by the losing side were simply a slightly amplified version of the typical sulky-toddler behavior we saw from Republicans after the election of Barack Obama in 2008 and Democrats after the election of George W. Bush in 2000. I honestly expected that the Democrats, once they'd gotten over the ritual period of wailing in anguish because they'd lost the White House, would pick themselves up, learn from the manifold mistakes that their candidate made during the campaign, and figure out why a significant number of voters who normally sided with them had taken their chances on Donald Trump instead.

That didn't happen. Not only did the tantrums keep coming, they turned more shrill and surreal with each passing week. What's more, not only did the Democrats fail to learn from their many mistakes, they doubled down on them, angrily rejecting any suggestion that would help them make sense of why they lost the election and keep them from doing the same thing over again. People watching from the sidelines, with various blends of astonishment and mordant glee, began talking about "Trump Derangement Syndrome." Meanwhile Trump began to use the overreactions of his opponents as an instrument of political warfare, bombarding the internet with carefully timed Twitter salvoes to keep his critics distracted while he carried out the most dramatic reshaping of the American governmental landscape in living memory. It really did look at times as though Trump's opponents were under some kind of magic spell.

In a certain sense, of course, that's exactly what was going on. I say "in a certain sense" because it's very difficult to talk about magic in modern industrial society and be understood clearly. That's not because magic is innately difficult to understand. It's because our culture has spent the last two thousand years or so doing its level best not to understand it.

Magic is the art and science of causing changes in consciousness in accordance with will. Let's repeat that and give it due emphasis: *magic is the art and science of causing changes in consciousness in accordance with will.* That's the definition proposed a century ago by Dion Fortune, an influential twentieth-century theoretician of magic (and also a crackerjack practitioner). Yes, I know that's not how magic is presented in the corporate mass media, and there are good reasons for that. The babblings of the corporate mass media don't matter, though, because that definition is how magic is understood by many of the people who actually do it.

But what about the robes and candles and wands, the billowing clouds of incense, the sonorous words of power, the strange glyphs drawn on talismans or held intently in the mind's eye? Those are tools for, ahem, causing changes in consciousness in accordance with will. The rational mind, the most recently evolved part of our cognitive equipment and far and away the most fragile, occupies only a small and relatively feeble corner of human consciousness. The rest still speaks the old vivid language of myth and symbol, and can be reached by dramatic action focused on nonrational clusters of symbolism—that is to say, by ritual and other magical practices—far more effectively than it can be reached by verbal reasoning.

It doesn't matter whether or not you think there's anything super-natural going on in magical practices, by the way. It doesn't matter whether you think there's anything going on at all. Operative mages—people who practice magic—have been experimenting with these practices for many thousands of years. If you follow their instructions you can get the same results they do. That's why people in every human society in history have practiced magic, and why plenty of people practice magic in the modern industrial world right now.

I'm one of them. In my early teens, bored out of my wits by the tacky plastic tedium of an American suburban existence, I went looking for something—anything—less dreary than the simulacrum of life that parents, teachers, and the omnipresent mass media insisted I ought to enjoy. Since I was a socially awkward bookworm—the diagnosis "Asperger's syndrome" wasn't in wide circulation yet—that search focused on books rather than the drugs, petty crime, and casual promiscuity in which most of my peers took refuge. In among the flying saucers, werewolf legends, and Ripley's *Believe It or Not!* trivia, I began to notice references to magic: not as a plot engine in fairy stories and fantasy novels, but as something that people actually did. One hint led to another, and eventually to books on the subject. By the time I was sixteen I'd begun experimenting with magical rituals and discovered that they do indeed work—that is, done correctly, they cause change in consciousness in accordance with will. Not long after my twenty-second birthday I began the kind of systematic program of study and practice that in magic, as in anything else, is necessary if you want to get past the bunny-slope level.

That was more than thirty-five years ago. Well before Donald Trump began his journey to the White House. In other words, I knew my way around the theory and practice of magic, and I also had a fair grasp of its history. I'd written quite a few books on magic and also translated or edited some of the major classics in the field. I'd put many hours of close study into books such as Ioan Couliano's *Eros and Magic in the Renaissance,* with its edgy but accurate identification of modern advertising as a debased form of magic, and Nicholas Goodrick-Clarke's *The Occult Roots of Nazism,* which got past the haze of mythmaking that has surrounded that subject since 1945 to show how a subculture of reactionary occultists in Germany and Austria laid the foundations for the coming of National Socialism. I'd also read and reread Carl Jung's prophetic essay "Wotan," written in 1936, which challenged the casual dismissal of Hitler as a two-bit Mussolini wannabe—yes, that's what serious people thought of him then—and showed how the Nazi movement fed on irrational forces rooted in the deep places of the European mind.

Donald Trump isn't Hitler. The newborn populist movement, which helped put him into office, backed him straight through his term in spite of all the efforts of the political establishment and the corporate media, and remains a massive presence in American public life despite the outcome of the 2020 election, has very little in common with the movement Hitler led to a string of sordid triumphs ending in catastrophe. Yet the huge and passionate crowds in red MAGA caps who flooded stadiums to hear Trump speak signal the presence of something other than the scripted faux-enthusiasm of politics as usual in the United States. The debased magic of modern political advertising has slammed face first into something older, deeper, and far less reasonable, and the shockwaves from the impact are leaving few of our culture's comforting certainties intact.

That was what I saw taking shape in late 2015, as Donald Trump emerged from the pack of Republican presidential candidates, and the entire political landscape of the United States began to warp around him like spacetime twisting around a neutron star. That's what I've watched since then, as we've moved further and further into an unfamiliar world where the regular rules no longer apply and strange shapes rise from the depths.

When you practice magic you get used to encountering the bizarrely meaningful coincidences that Carl Jung called "synchronicities." You do a ritual invoking the forces assigned to the planet Mars, whose symbols include the color red and the number five, and when you walk to the grocery an hour later the only vehicles that pass you are five bright red cars: that sort of thing. At the same time as the Trump phenomenon was beginning to take shape, I had a classic example of the sort show up on my doorstep—or more precisely on my keyboard.

Among the many things I read back in my teen years in search of alternatives to boredom was the fiction of iconic American weird-tales author H. P. Lovecraft. Most people think of Lovecraft as a horror writer, but I never found his stories scary. The tentacle-faced devil-god Cthulhu, the shapeless shoggoths, and the other critters who inhabit his adjective-laden pages never struck me as particularly horrifying. Me, I found them oddly endearing, and they were certainly better company than most of the people I knew.

Lovecraft was a passing phase for me, though I returned to his stories in the years that followed. Then in the spring of 2015—yes, right about the time that Donald Trump launched himself into the presidential race—I suddenly had a fantasy novel come crashing into my imagination, set in a quirky reimagining of Lovecraft's fictive cosmos in which his monsters and gods were the good guys, their supposedly sinister cultists turned out to be just one more religious minority targeted by hateful propaganda and violent persecution, and the villains of the piece belonged to a vast and powerful organization of crazed rationalists who wanted to turn all that rhetoric about Man's Conquest of Nature into an ecocidal reality. Eight weeks later—I have never written anything else so fast or with so few missteps—I had a 70,000-word first draft of *The Weird of Hali: Innsmouth,* the first installment of what turned into a seven-volume epic fantasy with tentacles, accompanied by four equally tentacular novels, which took place in the same eldritch setting.

As the rest of the series began to take shape, I saturated myself in classic weird tales from before the Second World War: Lovecraft's to begin with, and then those of the writers he admired or befriended. I borrowed freely from a great many of those to fill out the fictive landscape of *The Weird of Hali,* and in the process began to notice just how precisely the world seemed to be following in the footsteps of my fiction. Sometimes the resonances were exact. I borrowed the toad god Tsathoggua from the stories of Lovecraft's friend Clark Ashton Smith, for example, and within a week heard for the first time of the sudden prominence of the frog god Kek in the online subculture of the alt-right. Equally, a few years later on, these lines from Robert W. Chambers' book *The King in Yellow* took on new relevance in the age of Covid-19:

STRANGER: I wear no mask.
CAMILLA: [*terrified, aside to Cassilda*] No mask? No mask!

Even so, the general ambience seems even more significant than such details. As in Lovecraft's story "The Call of Cthulhu" and a hundred other weird tales, something vast and dreadful was stirring in the depths, gathering strength from among those that the respectable dismissed as the dregs of society, haunting the dreams of a world that believed that all such primeval horrors had been laid to rest forever.

Of all the classic weird tales I read while working on *The Weird of Hali,* the ones that seemed to catch the flavor of our time most precisely were the linked short stories Robert W. Chambers gathered in *The King in Yellow.* Most of those stories are set in the ordinary world of Chambers' time, but prosaic reality begins to twist and shudder as a different reality seeps through the crawlspaces: the reality of Carcosa, the city of the King in Yellow, where the shadows of thought lengthen in the afternoon and black stars hang in the heavens. That same vertiginous sense of shifting realities, it seemed to me, has been spreading throughout American public life in the age of Trump, and the madness that played so central and disquieting a role in Chambers' stories was there in ample supply as well. The one great difference I could see was that the force warping the political and cultural landscape of our time had orange rather than yellow for its keynote color. The titles of this book and its chapters, and much of the imagery that shapes the following pages, followed promptly.

✳

A word of caution is in order before we begin. For those readers who've bought into the narratives pushed by the corporate media and its tame pundits for the past forty years or so, this book won't be easy reading. To make sense of the Trump phenomenon and the magical politics that made Trump's ascent to the presidency inevitable, we'll have to look clearly at the realities of social class and class prejudice in today's America, the consequences of policies that have been treated as sacrosanct by the people who benefited from them most, and the ways that rhetorics of moral superiority have been weaponized to justify those policies and stifle dissent. We'll have to talk frankly about the nature of history and the contemporary cult of progress, and glimpse the shape of a future that has little in common with the cheapjack Tomorrowland imagery the mass media has been pushing so frantically at us for so many years.

What makes these things difficult for most people nowadays is not that they're unfamiliar. Quite the contrary, they rouse such strong emotional reactions because we all know them already. They're the tacit realities we live with every day but most of us never dare to mention or even think about, as unavoidable as they are unspeakable—and they're the reasons why Donald Trump became president of the United States.

Ever since the 2016 election, it has been fashionable in the cultural mainstream to insist that Trump was an anomaly. Deep down we all know better. Trump was anything but an anomaly. His election in 2016 was the necessary result of forty years of policies that benefited certain classes in our society at the expense of others, while tacitly forbidding any discussion of that fact. The populist movement that came together in response to his candidacy and is now beginning to take its first independent steps grew partly out of the reaction to those policies, partly out of a schism in America's culture and consciousness that goes all the way back to colonial times, and partly out of something far more inchoate that reaches not back but forward: the first stirrings of a distant future within the hard shell of the present.

These are the realities we most need to grapple with today. To borrow and repurpose a metaphor from Chambers' stories, we've seen the Orange Sign, and there's no way back from that moment of revelation. We can close our eyes to our own knowledge and be blindsided by the future, or we can open our eyes and see the world that's beginning to take shape around us. This book is my attempt at that first necessary glance.

1

A Season in Carcosa

The Political Dimensions of Magic

This is the thing that troubles me, for I cannot forget Carcosa where black stars hang in the heavens; where men's thoughts lengthen in the afternoon, when the twin suns sink into the Lake of Hali; and my mind will bear for ever the memory of the Pallid Mask.

FROM "THE REPAIRER OF REPUTATIONS"
IN *THE KING IN YELLOW*

Like millions of other Americans on November 8, 2016, I took part in the pleasant civic ritual of electing a president. My polling place at that time was in an elementary school in a rundown neighborhood of Cumberland, Maryland, a gritty, impoverished, and rather pleasant town of 20,000 people in the north central Appalachians, and I walked there early that afternoon, when the lunch rush was over and the torrent of people voting on the way home from work hadn't gotten under way. There was no line at the polling place. I went in just as two old men came out the door, comparing notes on which local restaurants gave discounts to patrons who wear the "I Voted" stickers that polling places hand out, and left five minutes later as a bottle-blonde housewife in her fifties came in to cast her vote. Maryland had electronic voting for a while, but did the smart thing and went back to paper ballots that year, so I'm pretty sure my votes got counted the way I cast them.

The weather was cloudy but warm, as nice a November day as you could ask for, and the streets I walked down were typical of the poorer parts of flyover country: every third house abandoned, every third street corner hosting an off-brand church. It's the kind of neighborhood where, on a warm summer evening, all the porches have people sitting on them, and despite the stereotypes you'll hear endlessly repeated in the corporate media, you'll have to look long and hard to find even one of those porches where everyone tipping back a beer has the same skin color. The kids playing basketball in the rundown playground close by are just as complete an ethnic mix, and interracial marriages and mixed-race children are common in that part of town.

That afternoon, as I went to vote and then returned, that impoverished, rundown, ebulliently multiracial neighborhood was also an unbroken forest of pro-Trump signage. Trump's name and his slogan "Make America Great Again" were everywhere. And Clinton? If you wanted to see any of her signs you had to walk uphill to a different part of town. That way lies one of Cumberland's few well-to-do neighborhoods, where you won't see friends tipping back beers on porches or mixed-race couples walking down the street holding hands. That's where you found the Clinton campaign signs—"I'm With Her"—on that pleasant November afternoon. They were with her. The working-class people down the hill, struggling to get by after decades of increasingly bleak times in America's flyover states, were with Trump.

That wasn't the way the corporate media or the comfortable classes presented the contest, of course. After that November day, and especially once the shock of Hillary Clinton's defeat settled in, the conventional wisdom insisted loudly that every single person who voted for Donald Trump must have been motivated by racism, sexism, or some other form of socially unacceptable prejudice, and could not possibly have had any other reason for voting that way. The same media outlets and affluent circles insisted just as stridently that Trump had colluded with the government of Russia to rig the election, or simply blamed Trump's victory on hate, as though that unfashionable emotion had done the thing all by itself. You heard these claims rehashed across a broad slide of the political spectrum, from the far left through the center to the "Never Trump" wing of the Republican Party—from everyone, in short, but the people who voted for Trump, or those who took the time to listen to them and find out what they thought.

To some extent, of course, this was yet another round of the amateur theatrics that both parties indulge in whenever they lose the White House. In 2008, Barack Obama's victory was followed by months of shrieking from Republicans, who insisted that the outcome of the election meant that democracy had failed, the United States and the world were doomed, and Republicans would be rounded up and sent to concentration camps any day now. In 2000, Democrats chewed the scenery in a comparably grand style when George W. Bush was elected president. In 1992, it was the GOP's turn—I still have somewhere a pamphlet circulated by Republicans after the election containing helpful phrases in Russian, so that American citizens would have at least a little preparation when Bill Clinton ran the country into the ground and handed the smoking remains over to the Soviet Union. (Yes, I'm old enough to remember when Republicans rather than Democrats were finding sinister Russians under the bed.) American politics and popular culture being what they are, this kind of histrionic silliness is probably unavoidable.

Fans of irony had at least as much to savor in 2016 as in these earlier examples. We saw people who were talking eagerly about how to game the Electoral College two weeks before the election, who turned around and started denouncing the Electoral College root and branch once it cost their party the presidency. We saw people who had insisted that Trump, once he lost, should concede and shut up, who demonstrated a distinct unwillingness to follow their own advice once the shoe was on the other foot. We saw people in the bluest of blue left-coast cities marching in protest as though that was going to change a single blessed thing, since protest marches that aren't backed up with effective grassroots political organization are simply a somewhat noisy form of aerobic exercise.

Still, more was involved than theatrical posturing. A great many people on the losing side of the election reacted with genuine feelings of shock, disorientation, and fear. At least some of them believed whole-heartedly that the people who voted for Trump hated women, people of color, sexual minorities, and so on, and could have been motivated only by that hatred. What was more, that belief became more deeply entrenched, not less, as people who had actually voted for Trump tried to explain why it was wrong, and it became even more widespread after Trump took office and failed to do the extreme things his opponents insisted he was going to do, and pursued a series of policies that, as we will see, benefited a great many Americans who had been left behind or actively harmed by the much-ballyhooed policies of previous administrations.

Were there people among Trump's supporters who were racists, sexists, homophobes, and so on? Of course. I knew a couple of thoroughly bigoted racists who cast their votes for him, for example, including at least one bona fide member of the Ku Klux Klan. The point the Left ignored, and has insisted on ignoring ever since, is that not everyone in flyover country is like that. A few years before the election, in fact, a group of Klansmen came to Cumberland to hold a recruitment rally, and the churches in town—white as well as black—held a counter-rally on the other side of the street and drowned the Klansmen out, singing hymns at the top of their lungs until the guys in the white robes got back in their cars and drove away in humiliation. Surprising? Not at all; in a great deal of Middle America, that's par for the course these days.

To understand why a town that ran off the Klan gave Donald Trump 70 percent of its vote in the 2016 election, it's necessary to get past the stereotypes and ask a simple question: Why did people vote for Trump in 2016? I spent a lot of time listening to people talk about the election before and after it happened, and these are the things they brought up over and over again.

1. *The Risk of War.* This was the most common point at issue, especially among women—nearly all the women I know who voted for Trump, and I know quite a few of them, cited it as either the decisive reason for their vote or one of the top two. They listened to Hillary Clinton talk about imposing a no-fly zone over Syria in the face of a heavily armed and determined Russian military presence, and looked at the reckless enthusiasm for overthrowing governments she'd displayed during her time as Secretary of State. They compared this to Donald Trump's advocacy of a less confrontational relationship with Russia, and they decided that Trump was less likely to get the United States into a shooting war.

War isn't an abstraction in flyover country. Joining the military is very nearly the only option young people there have if they want a decent income, job training, and the prospect of a college education, and so most families have at least one relative or close friend on active duty. People respect the military. Even so, the last two decades of wars of choice in the Middle East have done a remarkably good job of curing Middle America of any fondness for military adventurism it might have had. While affluent feminists swooned over the prospect of a woman taking on another traditionally masculine role, and didn't seem to care in the least that the role in question was "warmonger," a great many people in flyover country weighed the other issues against the prospect of having a family member come home in a body bag. Since the Clinton campaign did nothing to reassure them on this point, they voted for Trump.

2. *The Obamacare Disaster.* This was nearly as influential as Clinton's reckless militarism. Most of the people I know who voted for Trump made too much money to qualify for a significant federal subsidy, and too little to be able to cover the endlessly rising cost of insurance under the absurdly misnamed "Affordable Care Act." They recalled, too clearly for the electoral prospects of the Democrats, how Obama assured them that the price of health insurance would go down,

that they would be able to keep their existing plans and doctors, and so on through the other broken promises that surrounded Obamacare even before it took effect.

It was bad enough that so few of those promises were kept, and that millions of Americans lost health coverage that met their needs at a reasonable price and instead got poorer coverage with drastically higher premiums. The real dealbreaker, though, was the round of double- or triple-digit annual increases in premiums announced just before the election, on top of increases nearly as drastic a year previously. Even among those who could still afford the new premiums, the writing was on the wall: sooner or later, unless something changed, a lot of people were going to have to choose between losing their health care and being driven into destitution—and then there were the pundits who insisted that everything would be fine, if only the penalties for not getting insurance were raised to equal the cost of insurance! Faced with that, it's not surprising that a great many people went out and voted for the one candidate who said he'd get rid of Obamacare.

3. *Bringing Back Jobs.* This is the most difficult issue for a great many people on the Left to understand. In flyover country, the great-granddaddy of economic issues is access to full time working-class jobs at decent pay. Such jobs used to be readily available in cities, towns, and rural areas across the country, back when government regulation was modest, substantial tariffs and trade barriers protected domestic manu-facturing industries, and immigration was strictly regulated. As each of these policies was reversed, wages dropped and jobs became more scarce. Until quite recently, every respectable mainstream economist insisted heatedly that the plunge in working-class wages and the decrease in job availability had nothing to do with the policy changes just listed. A great many people in Middle America didn't believe them—and there was reason for their skepticism.

All through the campaign, Clinton pushed the bipartisan consensus that supported more regulation, more free trade agreements, and more immigration. Trump, by contrast, promised to cut regulation, scrap or renegotiate free trade agreements, and crack down on illegal immigration. He was the only candidate who offered something other than a continuation of existing policies, and that was enough to get a good many voters whose economic survival was on the line to take a chance on Trump.

4. *Punishing the Democratic Party.* This one is more of an outlier, because the people I know who cast their votes for Trump for this reason mostly represented a different demographic from the norm in flyover country: younger, politically more liberal, and incensed by the way that the Democratic National Committee rigged the nomination process to favor Clinton and shut out Bernard Sanders. They believed that if the campaign for the Democratic nomination had been conducted fairly, Sanders would have been the nominee, and they also believed that Sanders would have stomped Trump in the general election. For what it's worth, my guess is that they were right on both counts.

These voters pointed out to me, often with some heat, that the policies Hillary Clinton supported in her time as senator and secretary of state were all but indistinguishable from those of George W. Bush—that is, the policies Democrats used to denounce so forcefully back before they themselves started pursuing them. These voters argued that voting for Clinton in the general election when she'd been rammed down the throats of the Democratic rank and file by the party's oligarchy would have signaled the final collapse of the party's progressive wing into irrelevance. They were willing to accept four years of a Republican in the White House to make it brutally clear to the party hierarchy that the shenanigans that handed the nomination to Clinton were more than they were willing to tolerate.

Those were the reasons I heard people give when they talked about why they were voting for Donald Trump. They didn't talk about the issues that the corporate media considered important, such as the shenanigans around Hillary Clinton's private email server. Nor did they display any particular hatred toward women, people of color, sexual minorities, and the like; many of them *were* women, people of color, and/or sexual minorities—despite stereotypes common in the coastal enclaves of the comfortable, Cumberland not only has the ethnic mix I discussed earlier, it has a gay bar and an annual drag queen pageant. The Trump voters here had their own reasons, which I've listed above.

When this was pointed out to people on the leftward side of the political spectrum, the usual response has been to insist that, well, yes, maybe Trump did address the issues that matter to people in flyover country, but even so, it was utterly wrong of them to vote for a racist, sexist homophobe! We'll set aside the question of how far these labels actually apply to Trump, and how much they're the product of demonizing rhetoric on the part of his political enemies. Even accepting the truth of these accusations, what the line of argument just cited claims is that people in the flyover states should have ignored the issues that affect their own lives, and should have voted instead for the issues that liberals think are important.

In some idyllic Utopian world, maybe. In the real world, that's not going to happen. People are not going to embrace the current agenda of the American Left if that means they can expect their medical insurance to double in price every few years, their wages to continue lurching downward, their communities to sink further in a death spiral of economic collapse, and their kids to come home in body bags from another pointless war in the Middle East. That anyone should have thought otherwise is a helpful measure of the strangeness of our times, and points straight to the deeper, magical dimensions of contemporary politics.

One of the fascinating things about all this is that the issues just listed are all things the Democratic Party used to address. It wasn't that long ago, in fact, that the Democratic Party made these very issues—opposition to reckless military adventurism, support for government programs that improved the standard of living of working-class Americans, and a politics of transparency and integrity—central not only to its platform but to the legislation it fought to get passed and its presidents signed into law. Back when that was the case, the Democratic Party was the majority party in this country, not only in Congress but also in terms of state governorships and legislatures. As the party backed away from offering those things, in turn, it lost its majority position. While correlation doesn't prove causation, I think that this once a strong case can be made.

Nor was it especially difficult to find out that the things listed above were the issues that American voters cared about, and that they voted for Trump because he seemed more likely to provide them than Clinton did. Yet across this country's collective conversation in the wake of the election, next to no one other than Trump voters wanted to hear it. Suggest that people voted for Trump because they were worried about the risk of war, afraid that Obamacare would bankrupt their families, hoping a change in policy would bring back full-time jobs at decent wages, or disgusted by the political trickery that kept Sanders from winning the Democratic nomination, and you could count on being shouted down. It became an item of unshakable dogma in the media and the realm of public discourse that every single one of the voters who supported Trump could only have been motivated by sheer evil.

To understand that bizarre but pervasive reaction is to plunge into the heart of what happened in the 2016 U.S. presidential election. The conventional wisdom offers no guidance here. Instead, the route to understanding begins with a corpse in a bathroom.

The bathroom in question was on the University of Chicago campus, on an otherwise lovely spring day in 1991. The corpse belonged to Ioan Couliano, a Romanian-American historian of ideas who had earned a stellar reputation for a series of books on the odder byways of Renaissance thought. Couliano had been shot once in the head by an unknown assailant. It remains an open case, though the victim had been heavily involved in attempts to unseat the regime that took power in Romania after the Communist collapse in 1989, and rumors then and now attribute the killing to that regime's security forces.

We'll be returning to Couliano's career and grisly death more than once in the pages ahead. The aspect of his work that concerns us just now is his 1984 book *Eros and Magic in the Renaissance,* which cut straight through modern misunderstandings of magic to show how it has become the basis of political power in the modern industrial world. Though this wasn't widely known until after his death, Couliano was a practitioner of magic as well as an academic; he had made a close study of the magical writings of Giordano Bruno, a defrocked Dominican friar who was burnt at the stake for heresy in 1600, and that background gave him the key to understand the magical politics of the present day.

The most important of Giordano Bruno's magical writings, *De Vinculis in Genere (On Bindings in General),* identified desire—*eros,* in Bruno's Latin prose—as the key to magic. Look at today's mass-media advertising, Couliano pointed out, and everything you see is meant to manipulate consciousness through images that evoke desire. Advertising and public relations are the magic of today: that was one of Couliano's core messages.

Yet that identification of advertising as magic led him to further insights. From his perspective, authoritarian regimes of the old-fashioned jackbooted kind were anachronisms in today's world. The nations of the modern industrial West need nothing so clumsy to maintain conformity and keep the existing order of things from being disturbed, when advertising and public relations can do the same job ever so much more efficiently. *Eros and Magic in the Renaissance* thus presented an edgy vision of modern industrial societies as "magician states" in which the mass media maintains an artificial consensus that supports existing distributions of power and wealth by tacitly excluding all alternatives.

There's much to be said for Couliano's interpretation, and several other equally subversive currents of thought have made the same point in their own way. The most important thing being sold by an advertisement, after all, is not the product it ostensibly promotes, but the set of beliefs and attitudes that makes the product seem desirable. An ad for fizzy brown sugar water, say, wastes no time extolling the notional virtues of fizzy brown sugar water; instead, it cycles obsessively through images meant to evoke desires for love, friendship, popularity, or what have you, and linking those desires to the consumption of fizzy brown sugar water. Underlying the whole ad is the claim that people who want love, friendship, popularity, or what have you can get it by buying a product. The mere fact that this belief is obviously false, and indeed absurd, does nothing to decrease its impact on the unthinking.

The power of such imagery is undeniable. Yet there was always a problem, a severe one, with Bruno's approach to magic, and with Couliano's interpretation of that approach. Both men, it bears remembering, ended up messily dead, and in both cases that happened because the magical manipulations in which they put their trust turned out to be less potent than they thought: Bruno's incantations failed to keep him out of the hands of the Inquisition, while Couliano's brought him lethal blowback from the regime he tried to destabilize. As we'll see, the standard political discourse in the United States came to rely just as heavily on the manipulation of desire as the marketing of any other pre-packaged product, and failed in the same way as Bruno's and Couliano's rather different campaigns. All things considered, Hillary Clinton was lucky to get off as easily as she did.

Study the early stages of the 2016 presidential campaign and you can see Couliano's style of magic in high relief. That campaign started out as equivalent campaigns here in the United States have done for years, with carefully scripted campaign launches by political insiders who avoided the issues that actually mattered to most voters and fixated instead on advertising of exactly the sort we've been discussing. Jeb Bush, who was expected to take the Republican nomination and go head to head with Hillary Clinton in the general election, offers a good first approximation of the whole process, because his campaign was a letter-perfect copy of the successful presidential campaigns of the past three decades.

Bush really did do everything he was supposed to do, according to the conventional wisdom of the pre-Trump era, and according to the approach to magic Bruno and Couliano discussed. He lined up plenty of big-money sponsors; he assembled a team of ghostwriters, spin doctors, and door-to-door salesmen to run his campaign; he had a PR firm design a catchy logo; he practiced spouting the kind of empty rhetoric that sounds meaningful so long as you don't think about it for two minutes; he took carefully calculated stands on a handful of hot-button topics, mouthed whatever his handlers told him to say on every other issue, and set out to convince the voters that their interests would be harmed just a little bit less by putting him in the White House than by any of the alternatives.

That sort of content-free campaign is what got George H. W. Bush, Bill Clinton, George W. Bush, and Barack Obama onto the list of U.S. presidents. What it got Jeb Bush, though, was a string of humiliating defeats. Some observers at the time suggested that his tearful exit from the race in the wake of the South Carolina primary was the act of a child who had been promised a nice shiny presidency by his daddy, and then found out that the mean voters wouldn't give it to him. I think, though, that there was considerably more to it than that. I think that Bush had just realized, to his shock and horror, that the rules of the game had been changed on him without notice, and all those well-informed, well-connected people who had advised him on the route that would take him to the presidency had been smoking their shorts.

If anything, though, Hillary Clinton's 2016 campaign offers an even clearer glimpse into the magical dimensions of the American political process. She did exactly the same things that Jeb did—it's indicative that the two of them both splashed their first names across their equally banal campaign logos—and she also managed, as he never did, to get the apparatchiks of her party lined up solidly on her side before the campaigning season got under way. By the ordinary rules of U.S. politics, she should have enjoyed a leisurely stroll through the primaries to the Democratic convention while Jeb Bush wrestled with his opponents, and then gone into the general election with plenty of money to spare, saturating the air waves with a deluge of nearly content-free advertisements designed to associate her, in the minds of American voters, with a set of desires just a little more appealing than those her opponent was able to deploy.

But the rules had changed. Bernard Sanders staged a brilliantly effective challenge against Clinton's march to her coronation, and only lost the nomination because Democratic Party insiders pulled every dirty trick they knew to bias the process against him. Then, instead of going up against another bland insider in the kind of tepid race to the center that can easily be clinched by vacuous advertising, she had to face Donald Trump, who had seen off every other Republican candidate with contemptuous ease, and who proceeded to turn the same tactics that won him the nomination on the Clinton campaign with devastating effect.

Now of course Clinton made Trump's victory much easier than it had to be. All through the campaign, her attitude toward the election looked like nothing so much as what happens when someone puts money into a defective vending machine. She put in her quarter and pushed the right button, but the presidency didn't drop into her hands. The rest of her campaign can be best described as a matter of jabbing the button over and over again, and finally pounding on the thing and screaming at it because it wouldn't give Clinton the prize that she'd paid for. I honestly don't think she ever considered the possibility that the electorate might not simply be a passive mechanism that would spit up a presidency for her if she just manipulated it in the right way. Until the night of November 8, I doubt it entered her darkest dream that the American people might decide to cast their votes to further their own interests rather than hers.

That analysis seems plausible to me for a variety of reasons, but high among them is the way that Clinton's supporters among her own class-and-gender subcategory demanded that American women back the Clinton campaign for no reason at all. I'm thinking here particularly of Madeleine Albright, who made the news with an irate public statement insisting that "there's a special place in hell for women who don't help other women." That's a common trope among a certain well-paid class of Second Wave feminists. It's become controversial, and for good reason, among a great many other feminists, particularly in the partly overlapping sets of women of color and women in the working class. Listen to them, and you'll hear at some length how they feel about being expected to help rich and influential women like Madeleine Albright pursue their goals, when they know perfectly well the favor won't be returned in any way that matters.

What, after all, did a Clinton presidency offer the majority of American women, other than whatever vicarious rush of ersatz fulfillment they might get from having a female president? The economic policies Clinton espoused—the bipartisan consensus of the pre-Trump era, from which she showed no signs of veering in the slightest—blithely ignored the poverty and misery suffered by millions of American women who didn't happen to share her privileged background and more than ample income. Her tenure as Secretary of State was marked by exactly the sort of hamfisted interventions in other people's countries to which Democrats, once upon a time, used to object: interventions, please note, that were responsible for hundreds of thousands of deaths in Syria, Libya, and elsewhere. If Clinton took the same attitudes with her into the White House, a good many American women might well have faced the experience of watching their family members come home in body bags from yet another brutal and pointless Mideast war.

The reaction to Albright's public tantrum is in many ways as instructive as the tantrum itself. A great many American women simply didn't buy it. More generally, no matter how furiously Clinton and her flacks hammered on the buttons of the vending machine, trying to elicit the mechanical response they thought they could expect, the voters refused to fall into line and respond passively to the magical images dragged in front of them. Trump and Sanders, each in his own way, showed too many people that it's possible to hope for something other than business as usual. In their wake, a great many voters decided that they were no longer willing to vote for the lesser of two evils.

That's a point of some importance. To my mind, it's far from accidental that for the past few decades, every presidential election here in the United States has been enlivened by bumper stickers and buttons calling on voters to support the presidential ambitions of Cthulhu, the tentacled primeval horror featured in H. P. Lovecraft's tales of cosmic dread. I'm sorry to say that the Great Old One's campaign faces a serious constitutional challenge, as he was spawned on the world of Vhoorl in the twenty-third nebula and currently resides in the drowned corpse-city of R'lyeh, and as far as I know neither of these are U.S. territories. Still, his bids for the White House have gone much further than most other imaginary candidacies, and I've long thought that the secret behind that success is Cthulhu's campaign slogan: "Why settle for the lesser evil?"

The reason that this slogan reliably elicits laughter, in turn, is that the entire rhetoric of presidential politics in the United States for decades now has fixated on the claim that one party's pet stooge won't do anything quite as appalling as the other side's will, even though they all support the same policies and are bought and sold by the same interests. Over and over again, we've been told that we have to vote for whatever candidate this or that party has retched up, because otherwise the other side will get to nominate a Supreme Court justice or two, or get us into another war, or do something else bad. Any suggestion that a candidate might do something positive to improve the lot of ordinary Americans is dismissed out of hand as "unrealistic."

What Trump's election showed conclusively, in turn, was that the lesser-evil rhetoric and its fixation on "realistic" politics have passed their pull date. There are very good reasons for this. The pursuit of the lesser evil means that the best the American people are allowed to hope for is the continuation of the current state of things—that's what you get, after all, if your only talking points fixate on stopping things from getting worse—and for most Americans today, the current state of things is unbearable. Cratering wages and soaring rents, a legal environment that increasingly denies even basic rights to everybody but corporations and the rich, an economy rigged to load ever-increasing costs on working people while funneling all the benefits to those who already have too much—well, you can fill in the list as well as I can. If you don't happen to belong to the privileged classes, life in today's America is rapidly becoming intolerable, and the "realistic" politics that both parties have pursued with equal enthusiasm for decades are directly responsible for making it intolerable. Thus the reason that a large and growing number of ordinary working Americans are refusing to accept another rehash of the status quo this time around is that their backs are to the wall.

That's a situation that comes up reliably at a certain point in the history of every society. To make sense of that recurrent pattern, it will help to call on another thinker not often heard from these days, the German historian Oswald Spengler. A high school teacher by trade, dry and acerbic, he devoted his spare time over the course of several decades to a polymath's banquet of historical studies. Unlike most Western historians of his time, he didn't limit his studies to Europe and its dependencies: the politics of the League of Mayapan in preconquest Central America, the rise of gardening as one of the fine arts in Chinese society, the debates that shaped ancient Indian philosophy, all these and much more were grist for his mill.

We'll talk further on about Spengler's broader analysis and the unmentionable reasons why the favorite historian of the Beat poets has been consigned to oblivion today. The theme of his that needs discussion here is his analysis of the way that democracies die. Spengler argued that democracy suffers from a lethal vulnerability, which is that it has no defenses against the influence of money. Since most citizens are more interested in their own personal advantage than they are in the destiny of their nation, democracy turns into a polite fiction for plutocracy just as soon as the rich figure out how to buy votes, a lesson that rarely takes them long to learn.

The problem with plutocracy, in turn, is that it embodies the same fixation on personal advantage that gives it its entry to power, since the only goals that guide the rich in their plutocratic rule are personal wealth and gratification. Despite the foam-flecked ravings of econo-mists, furthermore, it simply isn't true that what benefits the very rich automatically benefits the rest of society as well. Quite the contrary, in the blind obsession with personal gain that drives the plutocratic sys-tem, the plutocrats generally lose track of the hard fact that too much profiteering can run the entire system into the ground. A democracy in its terminal years thus devolves into a broken society from which only the narrowing circle of the privileged derive any benefit. In due time, those excluded from that circle look elsewhere for leadership.

The result is what Spengler calls "Caesarism": the rise of charismatic leaders who discover that they can seize power by challenging the plu-tocrats, addressing the excluded majority, and offering the latter some hope that their lot will be improved. Fairly often the leaders who fig-ure this out come from within the plutocracy itself. Julius Caesar, who contributed his family name to Spengler's vocabulary, was a very rich man from an old-money Senatorial family, and he's far from the only example. In 1918, Spengler predicted that the first wave of Caesarism in the Western world was about to hit, that it would be defeated by the plutocrats, and that other, more successful waves would follow. He was dead right on the first two counts, and the 2016 election shows that the third prediction is coming true on schedule.

To a very real extent, Hillary Clinton's faltering presidential cam-paign is a perfect microcosm of what Spengler had in mind in his cold analysis of democracy *in extremis*. Her entire platform presupposed that the only policies the United States can follow are those that have been welded in place since the turn of the millennium. Those policies have not brought any of the good things their promoters insisted that they were going to bring. Another four years of the same policies weren't going to change that fact. Every American voter knew as much, and so did Hillary Clinton, which is why her campaign focused on everything but the issues that concerned the majority of American voters. That's what lent a savage irony to Madeleine Albright's brittle insistence that American women had to support Clinton even though, for all practical purposes, she was offering them exactly what they got from George W. Bush. Albright's was the voice of a senile plutocracy on its way down, demanding a loyalty from others that it has done nothing to earn.

We got to see plenty of the same sort of irony as the election lurched toward its end. Clinton and her flacks kept on trying to reintroduce her to voters who already knew her quite well enough, thank you; there were endless encomiums about what a nice person she is—as though that mattered one jot to people who knew that four more years of the policies she supported might well have landed them out of a job and out on the street. Facile claims that everything was fine, the economy was booming, and the American people were happier than they had been in decades spread through the mass media. No doubt things looked that way to those who lived in a bubble of privilege, and took good care never to step outside it and see how the other 80 percent live. For that matter, it's true that if you take the obscene gains raked in by the privileged few and average them out across the entire population, that looks like economic betterment—but those gains were not being shared by the entire population, and outside the comfortable classes, at least, the entire population knew this perfectly well.

That was where Donald Trump came in. In his own way, the man is brilliant, and I say that without the least trace of sarcasm. He figured out very early in his campaign for the nomination that the most effective way to rally voters to his banner was to get himself attacked, in the usual tones of shrill mockery, by the defenders of the status quo. The man had the money to pay for the kind of hairstyle that the salary class finds acceptable, to cite an obvious example. He deliberately chose otherwise, because he knew that every time the media trotted out another round of insults directed at his failure to conform to the fashions of the privileged, another hundred thousand working-class voters recalled the sneering putdowns they experienced from their supposed betters and thought, "Trump's one of us."

The identical logic governed his deliberate flouting of the current rules of acceptable political discourse, before and after the election. Every time Trump tweeted something that sent the pundits into a swivet, and the media set out to convince itself and its listeners that this time he'd gone too far and his campaign or his presidency would surely collapse in humiliation, his poll numbers went up. What he says, you see, is the sort of thing that you'll hear people say in taverns and bowling alleys when subjects such as political corruption, media dishonesty, illegal immigration, and Muslim jihadi terrorism come up for discussion. The shrieks of the media simply confirm, in the minds of the voters to whom his appeal is aimed, that he's one of them, an ordinary Joe with sensible ideas who's being dissed by the suits.

Notice also how many of Trump's early rounds of unacceptable-to-the-pundits comments focused with laser precision on the issue of immigration. That was a well-chosen opening wedge, as cutting off illegal immigration is something that the GOP has claimed to support for many years. As Trump broadened his lead during the campaign, in turn, he started to talk about another side of the equation, the offshoring of jobs by U.S.-based corporations. The corporate media response did a fine job of proving his case: "If smartphones were made in the United States, we'd have to pay more for them!" Of course that's true: the comfortable classes will indeed have to pay more for their toys if working Americans are going to have jobs that pay enough to support a family. That this is unthinkable for so many people among the comfortable classes just named—that they're perfectly happy allowing their electronics to be made for starvation wages in overseas hellholes, so long as this keeps the price down—may help explain the boiling cauldron of resentment into which Trump tapped so efficiently.

Those points were crucial, because the issue at the heart of the 2016 election was whether the bipartisan consensus, which had been welded firmly in place in American politics since George W. Bush's first term, would stay intact. What set Donald Trump apart from nearly all the other candidates in the 2016 election was that he rejected core elements of that consensus: he called for an end to the federal policies that support offshoring of jobs, for the enforcement of U.S. immigration law, for sharp cuts in Federal regulation, and for a less rigidly confrontational stance toward Russia. To this day, Clinton's supporters insist that nobody actually cared about these issues, and that Trump's supporters were motivated by hateful values instead, but that rhetoric simply won't wash. The reason why Trump was able to sweep aside the other GOP candidates and then win the election despite the unanimous opposition of this nation's political class is precisely that he was the first presidential candidate in a generation to admit that the issues just mentioned actually matter.

That was a ticket to the nomination, in turn, because outside the bicoastal echo chamber of the affluent, the U.S. economy has spent decades in something close to freefall. The much-vaunted "recovery" of the Obama years benefited only the upper 20 percent or so by income of the population; the rest were left to get by on declining real wages, while having to face skyrocketing rents driven by federal policies that propped up the real estate market, and stunning increases in medical costs driven by the Affordable Care Act. It's no accident that death rates from suicide, drug overdose, and alcohol poisoning soared among working-class people. They were being driven to despair and destitution by a bipartisan policy consensus from which only Donald Trump was willing to dissent.

Most of the time, affluent liberals who are quick to emote about the sufferings of poor children and endangered species in conveniently distant corners of the Third World like to brush aside the issues I've just raised as irrelevancies. I long ago lost track of the number of times I've heard people insist that the American working class isn't suffering, that its suffering doesn't matter, or that the suffering was the fault of the working classes themselves. (I've occasionally heard people attempt to claim all three of these things at once.) On those occasions when the mainstream Left deigns to recognize the situation I've just sketched out, it's usually in the terms Hillary Clinton used in her famous "basket of deplorables" speech, in which she admitted that there were people who hadn't benefited from the recovery and "we need to do something for them." That the people in question might deserve to have a voice in what's done for them, or to them, is not part of the vocabulary of affluent Americans.

Glance at all this through the precisely adjusted lenses of Oswald Spengler's historical vision and the pattern is clear. Donald Trump is our Julius Caesar. How many people remember today that Caesar, rich as he was, was immensely popular with ordinary Romans, precisely because he spoke to them and for them against the interests of the immensely rich senatorial class that dominated the Roman Republic in its last century? Trump is just as popular because he fills the same historical role. The parallels are close enough that commenters on my blog early on took to referring to Trump as "the Orange Julius."

Spengler drew an important distinction between those aspects of history that follow repeating patterns and those that vary from one example to the next: in his melodramatic language, between Destiny and Incident. In the case of Julius Caesar, it was Incident that he happened to be the political figure who recognized that riding the populist backlash against a kleptocratic senatorial class could be his ticket to power, but it was Destiny that someone would do this and act on it. It was Incident that the backlash against him would take the form of an assassination plot, but it was Destiny that there would be a backlash of some kind. It was Incident that his nephew Octavius would pick up where he left off—it could as well have been Mark Antony, Pompey, or Julius Caesar himself, if he had escaped assassination—but it was Destiny that someone would do so. It was Incident that the result was the replacement of the Republic with an imperial monarchy, rather than a major reform of the Republic, but it was Destiny that something had to give.

In exactly the same way, the personalities of Donald Trump and his opponents, the tactics that won him the election and the very different tactics that lost it for Hillary Clinton, the machinations of the Democrats since 2016 and the details of how those machinations play out, and the broader magical context in which those tactics and machinations have their place, are all Incident in Spengler's sense of the term. What was Destiny was simply that sooner or later, an ambitious politician would figure out that addressing the concerns of the tens of millions whose voices had been shut out of the political conversation of our time was a ticket to power. Someone else would have done it if Trump hadn't. At this point, of course, the proverbial cat is out of the bag. A generation of rising politicians have taken note of his success and are prepared to duplicate it in other elections and, once he's gone, in the race for the presidency as well.

Trump's opponents haven't gotten that memo. As we'll see in the chapters to come, there's no way they could have gotten it, because their power depends on exactly the same willed blindness to the consequences of their preferred policies that Hillary Clinton displayed so colorfully all through her run for the presidency—a willed blindness that is the inescapable blowback from the style of magic she and they have used. It's thus an unshakable article of faith among Trump's foes that he has to be a temporary and incomprehensible aberration in the serene onward flow of a future that was supposed to give them everything they wanted. That conviction, too, is part of what Spengler would have called the Destiny of our times, and it set the stage for the magical politics of the 2016 election and the years that followed.

Magic, remember, is the art and science of causing change in consciousness in accordance with will. The 2016 election and its aftermath make the most sense when they're seen as a magical struggle between two parties of contending sorcerers. One party set out to summon certain unspeakable realities of American public life into visible appearance. The other party staked everything it had on an attempt to banish those same realities from sight forever. The two sides used radically different approaches to magic, and the success of one and the failure of the other unfolded from the mismatch between their approaches. Understand what those unspeakable realities are, how they reach down into the crawlspaces of American politics and culture, and how they made the mismatch of magical strategies inevitable, and you understand the history of our era.

2
Lengthening Shadows
Magic and the American Class System

In the desolate sky there was something that wearied, in the brooding clouds, something that saddened. It penetrated the freezing city by the freezing river. . . . A fine icy sleet was falling, powdering the pavement with a tiny crystalline dust. It sifted against the window-panes and drifted in heaps upon the sill. The light at the window had nearly failed, and the girl bent low over her work.

FROM "THE STREET OF THE FIRST SHELL"
IN *THE KING IN YELLOW*

Every society has a set of acceptable narratives that frame public discourse about any controversial subject. The main function of these narratives is to confine discourse on those subjects to approved channels, and those approved channels inevitably exclude crucial details and head off necessary questions. That isn't accidental; quite the contrary, it's their job, the core of what the narratives in question are meant to do. It is part of the magic by which the status quo maintains the illusion of its own inevitability and heads off challenges before they can even be thought clearly.

In today's United States, this is at least as true as elsewhere, and the saturation of our society by corporate advertising and public relations is among the major factors that make and keep it true. As a result, the facts concerning nearly every significant crisis we face can thus be divided up neatly into two entirely separate categories. The facts that most Americans are willing to talk about belong to one of these categories. The facts that matter belong to the other.

To understand the phenomenon of Donald Trump, in other words, we'll need to leave behind a great many common assumptions about our society. In particular, it's going to be necessary to ask my readers—especially, though not only, those who consider themselves liberals, or see themselves inhabiting some other position left of center in the convoluted landscape of American politics—to set aside a widespread but inaccurate belief: the notion that the only divisions in American society that matter are those that have some basis in biology. Skin color, gender, ethnicity, sexual orientation, disability—these are the lines of division in society that Americans like to talk about, whatever their attitudes to the people who fall on one side or another of those lines.

Please note, by the way, the four words above: "some basis in biology." I'm not saying that these categories are purely biological in nature. Every one of them is defined in practice by a galaxy of cultural constructs and presuppositions, and the link to biology is an ostensive category marker—a pointing finger, if you will—rather than a definition. I insert this caveat because I've noticed that a great many people go out of their way to misunderstand the point I'm trying to make here.

Are the lines of division just named important? Of course they are. Discriminatory treatment on the basis of those factors is a pervasive presence in American life today. The facts remain that there are other lines of division in American society that lack that anchor in biology, that some of these are at least as pervasive in American life as those listed above—and that some of the most important of these are taboo topics, subjects that most people in the United States today simply will not talk about.

Here's a relevant example. It so happens that you can determine a huge amount about the economic and social prospects of people in America today by asking one remarkably simple question: Where do they get most of their income? Broadly speaking—there are exceptions, to which I'll get in a moment—it's from one of four sources: returns on investment, a monthly salary with benefits, an hourly wage without benefits, or a government welfare check. People who get most of their income from one of those four things have a great many interests and experiences in common, so much so that it's meaningful to speak of the American people as divided into an investment class, a salary class, a wage class, and a welfare class.

It's probably necessary to point out explicitly here that these classes aren't identical to the divisions that Americans like to talk about. That is, there are plenty of people with light-colored skin in the welfare class, and plenty of people with darker skin in the wage class. Things tend to become a good deal more lily-white in the two wealthier classes, though even there you do find people of color. In the same way, women, gay people, disabled people, and so on are found in all four classes, and how they're treated depends a great deal on which of these classes they're in. If you're a disabled person, for example, your chances of getting mean-ingful accommodations to help you deal with your disability are by and large considerably higher if you bring home a salary than they are if you work for a wage.

As noted above, there are people who don't fall into those divisions. I'm one of them. As a writer, I get most of my income from royalties on book sales and subscriptions from my online writings, which means that a dollar or so from the sale of every book of mine gets mailed to me twice a year and a certain number of people send me $5 or $10 a month via the internet. There are so few people who make their liv-ing this way that the royalty-and-subscription classlet isn't a significant factor in American society. The same is true of most of the other ways of making a living in the United States today. Even the once-mighty profit class, the people who get their income from the profit they make on their own business activities, is small enough these days that it lacks a significant collective presence and thus any kind of political clout on the national level. The four categories I've listed above, by contrast, contain enough voters to matter.

There's a vast amount that could be said about the four major classes just outlined, but I want to focus on the political dimension, because that took on overwhelming relevance in the 2016 presidential campaign and its aftermath. Just as the four classes can be identified by way of a very simple question, the political dynamite that blew the certainties of American politics to smithereens in that election can be seen by way of another simple question: over the half century or so before the 2016 election, how did the four classes fare?

The answer, of course, is that three of the four have remained roughly where they were. The investment class has had some rough sailing, as many of the investment vehicles that used to provide it with stable incomes—certificates of deposit, government bonds, and so on—have seen interest rates drop through the floor in recent decades. Still, alternative investments and frantic government manipulations of stock market prices have allowed most people in the investment class to keep up their accustomed lifestyles.

The salary class, similarly, has maintained its familiar privileges and perks through a half century of convulsive change. Outside of a few coastal urban areas currently in the grip of speculative bubbles, people whose income comes mostly from salaries with benefits can generally afford to own their homes, buy new cars every few years, leave town for annual vacations, and so on. On the other end of the spectrum, the welfare class has continued to scrape by pretty much as before, dealing with the same bleak realities of grinding poverty, intrusive government bureaucracy, and a galaxy of direct and indirect barriers to full participation in the national life, that their equivalents had to confront back in 1966.

And the wage class? Over the half century leading up to 2016, the American wage class has been destroyed.

In 1966 an American family with one breadwinner working full time at an hourly wage could normally count on having a home, a car, three square meals a day, and the other ordinary necessities of life, with some left over for the occasional luxury. In 2016, an American family with one breadwinner working full time at an hourly wage was probably living on the street, and a vast number of people who would happily work full time even under those conditions could find only part-time or temporary work when they could find any jobs at all. The catastrophic impoverishment and immiseration of the American wage class is one of the most important political facts of our time—and it is also one of the most unmentionable. Until Trump, it was so thoroughly hedged about with magical spells that next to nobody was willing to talk about it, or even admit that it happened. Even today, it remains one of the least discussed issues in contemporary American life.

The destruction of the wage class was largely accomplished by way of three major shifts. The first was the dismantling of the industrial sector of the American economy and its replacement by imports from the Third World. The second was the tacit encouragement of mass illegal immigration from Third World countries. The third was the metastatic growth of government regulations that consistently benefited large corporations at the expense of small businesses. All three of these measures are, among other things, ways of driving down wages—not, please note, salaries, returns on investment, or welfare payments—by means of the law of supply and demand. Decrease the number of wage-paying jobs on the one hand, and increase the number of people competing for those jobs on the other, and wages on average go down: yes, it really is that simple.

It's probably going to be necessary to discuss these three factors in a little more detail, since a great deal of obfuscatory rhetoric has been deployed to confuse the issues surrounding them. Ever since David Ricardo first proposed the theory of free trade in the early nineteenth century, it has been a matter of blind faith among devout economists that free trade must be good for everyone, because it allows people in every country to specialize in whatever kind of economic activity they do best. In theory, maybe; in practice, since wages make up the bulk of production costs in the vast majority of industries, what happens is that jobs move to wherever wages and standards of living are lowest, driving down wages in countries with higher standards of living. This is why Britain's immense nineteenth-century economic boom time also featured the catastrophic impoverishment of the working classes that Charles Dickens chronicled so ably. It is also why U.S. manufacturing jobs shipped overseas were never replaced, despite easy promises made by politicians and pundits on both sides of the aisle.

U.S. immigration policy had the same effect in a different way. Under the policies in place up to 2016, legal immigration to the United States was relatively difficult but illegal immigration was easy. The result was the creation of an immense work force of noncitizens who had no legal rights they had any hope of enforcing, and who could be used by corporate interests—and were used, over and over again—to drive down wages, degrade working conditions, and advance the interests of employers over those of wage-earning employees.

The metastatic expansion of government regulation in the United States, finally, had the same effect in yet a third way. One of the reliable findings of economic research is that small businesses generate many more jobs per dollar of economic activity than large businesses. Federal regulations, in turn, systematically benefit large businesses at the expense of their smaller competitors in a galaxy of ways from the subtle to the blatant, and thus choke off one of the economy's prime engines of job creation for the wage class.

The next point that needs to be discussed here—and it's the one at which a very large number of my readers will likely balk—is who benefited most from the destruction of the American wage class. It has long been fashionable in what passed for American conservatism in the pre-Trump era to insist that everyone benefits from the changes just outlined, or to claim that if anybody doesn't, it's their own fault. It's been equally popular in what passes for American liberalism to insist that the only people who benefit from those changes are the villainous uber-capitalist running dogs who belong to the 1 percent. Both these are evasions because the destruction of the wage class has disproportionately benefited one of the four classes I sketched out above: the salary class.

Here's how that worked. Since the 1970s, the lifestyles of the salary class—suburban homeownership, a new car every few years, overseas vacations, and so on—have been an anachronism. They were only possible for a while because of the global economic dominance the United States wielded in the wake of the Second World War, when every other major industrial nation on the planet had its factories pounded to rubble by the bomber fleets of the warring powers, and the oil wells of Pennsylvania, Texas, and California pumped more oil than the rest of the planet put together. That dominance went away in a hurry, though, when U.S. conventional petroleum production peaked in 1970, and the factories of Europe and Asia began to outcompete America's industrial heartland.

The only way for the salary class to maintain the lavish lifestyles it preferred in the teeth of those transformations was to force down the cost of goods and services relative to their own buying power. Because the salary class exercised (and still exercises) a degree of economic and political influence disproportionate to its size, this became the order of the day in the 1970s, and it remained the locked-in political consensus in American public life until 2016. The destruction of the wage class was only one consequence of that project, but it's the consequence that matters most in terms of today's politics.

All this was possible because since the Second World War, the salary class has been in the ascendant across the industrial world. Read novels from before then, and it's taken for granted in such tales that what sets people apart as members of the privileged classes is the possession of enough investment income that they don't have to work. I'm thinking here, because it's a favorite book of mine, of Somerset Maugham's novel

The Razor's Edge. In the denouement, the detail that tells you that the protagonist Larry Darrell is on his way to a destiny most of the other characters can neither follow nor understand is that he has gotten rid of his investments, given the money away, and thus irrevocably removed himself from among the self-proclaimed Good People of his era.

If Maugham were writing today, Darrell's quest for freedom would have had him quit a job with a seven-figure salary and an ample benefits package, because that's what marks you in today's world as one of the Good People, or in other words a member of the privileged end of the salary class. The ascendancy of the salary class explains why in 1920, the CEOs of major corporations were the obsequious lackeys of the boards of directors, while now it's the other way around. It's also why interest rates, the most basic measure of the returns that provide the investment class with their income, have spent so many years at rock-bottom levels. Members of the salary class borrow more money than they invest, and so benefit from low interest rates; members of the investment class invest more than they borrow. The level at which interest rates are set is thus a good first measure of the balance of power between the two classes.

The ascendancy of the salary class also explains why every proposal enacted to help the two less prosperous classes, to benefit the environment, or to solve any other problem you care to name, always benefits the salary class far more than it does the purported beneficiaries of the proposal. Consider the loudly ballyhooed claims of the last couple of decades that unemployed members of the wage class could get back on board the bandwagon of prosperity by going to college and getting job training. That didn't work out very well for the people who signed up for the student loans and took the classes—getting job training, after all, isn't helpful if the jobs for which you're being trained don't exist, and so a great many former wage earners finished their college careers with no better job prospects than they had before, and burdened with hundreds of thousands of dollars of student loan debt into the bargain. For the banks and colleges that pushed the loans and taught the classes, though, these programs were a cash cow of impressive scale, and the people who work for banks, colleges, and federal and state education bureaucracies are mostly members of the salary class.

This is also why the environmental reforms promoted by well-funded think tanks and corporate media outlets impose costs solely on farmers, coal miners, and other people outside the salary class, while the earth-wrecking behaviors of the salary class—the frequent-flyer miles, the long commutes in SUVs, the vacations in Puerto Vallarta or Mazatlan, the sprawling and nearly uninsulated McMansions that use as much electricity as a city block in eastern Europe or an entire town in Indonesia, and the rest of it—get a free pass. Any time you see an environmental protest that focuses on getting governments to do something, while neglecting the massive carbon footprints of the people involved in the protest, you're looking at a display of salary-class privilege. The same points can be made just as precisely of sprawling bureaucratic welfare systems that pay miserable benefits to their supposed beneficiaries but provide vast numbers of college graduates with salaries and benefits, and so on through the litany of covert privilege that defines so much of the social landscape of our era.

The ascendancy of the salary class was defended, as the ascendancy of any dominant class is normally defended, by the magical strategy made famous by Margaret Thatcher's notorious slogan "There Is No Alternative"—TINA for short. By redefining the collective conversation so that only one set of policies is thinkable, it's possible to prevent any discussion of alternatives even when the policies in question have disastrous consequences for a very large share of the population. That gambit works even if there's some degree of social mobility, so long as you make agreement with the policies in question one of the unwavering requirements for access to influence and wealth.

Educational systems are the usual venue for this filtering process. Whether you're in the Chinese Empire and aspire to influence and wealth through membership in the mandarinate, or in the British Empire and aspire to influence and wealth through membership in the imperial civil service, or in modern America and aspire to influence and wealth through membership in this or that corporate hierarchy, the same rule applies: your chance of fulfilling those aspirations depends on your unswerving allegiance to whatever set of ideas your superiors want you to have, which are in turn those that maintain your superiors in power.

This has been the case now for quite a while in the United States, and the nations of the industrial West more broadly. Among those who have wealth and influence as well as those who aspire to both, the approved range of political, economic, social, and cultural attitudes is very narrow and very rigidly defined. Those who are rich enough can get away with violating those norms from time to time, so long as none of their rivals decides to use their strayings as a weapon against them. Those less privileged, though, have to watch their every word and action, knowing that these are being watched by their rivals and superiors. The ones who pass that test, who have talents and skills their superiors value, and who also have a larger than usual helping of old-fashioned luck, can hope to enter the lower circles of our society's aristocracy.

That's what we're talking about, of course. "Aristocracy" isn't a word that sees much use in that context, but it has more than a little to teach. As the term itself implies—it comes from the Greek words *aristoi,* "the best," and *krateia,* "power, rule"—an aristocracy is a group of people who believe that they rule because they're better than everyone else. The sense in which they consider themselves better is subject to all the usual historical and cultural vagaries, of course, but as an aristocracy ripens, those vagaries give way to an interesting uniformity.

Consider the meanings of the words *noble* and *gentle* in today's English. Originally, those words meant simply "belonging to the upper class." Similarly, consider the meanings of the words *churl* and *villain* in today's English. Originally those words meant nothing more than "a member of the lower classes." Those details of linguistic history express the standard pattern just mentioned. Every aristocracy comes to believe that it's morally superior to the people it rules. Aristocrats inevitably think of themselves as the Good People, the morally virtuous people, and they just as inevitably work out an ornate code of virtue signaling that's used to communicate their notional goodness to others of their class, and to exclude the rabble.

This matter of exclusion is of high importance. Every aristocracy is defined by *who* it excludes, but tries to excuse that definition in terms of *what* it excludes. That's what underlies both the pervasive virtue signaling of today's comfortable classes and the constant shifts in which virtue signals are expected. Both these are essential to the function of virtue signals as *class* signals—ways by which those who belong to today's American aristocracy, or who aspire to that status, can make themselves stand apart from the deplorable masses.

Such signals have become of great importance due to recent shifts in the composition of America's aristocracy. Not much more than a century ago, the upper end of the social pyramid in this country was defined strictly by gender and ethnic markers: the highest circles of power were restricted to heterosexual men whose ancestors all came from northwestern Europe, whose cultural background was overwhelmingly Anglo-American, and who went on Sundays to the Episcopalian (or, more rarely, Methodist) church. That set of criteria for exclusion made other kinds of class signal less necessary—a detail that permitted some degree of variation in behavior and opinions among aristocrats and those who aspired to their status.

As times changed and the American aristocracy caught onto the dangers of excluding too many of the talented, the criteria of exclusion changed. Over the course of the twentieth century, political and cultural markers replaced ethnic and gender markers to a certain extent. While most of the people in the highest circles of power still bear a close resemblance to their equivalents in 1900—look at a group photo of the U.S. Senate some time—a modest trickle of women and ethnic minorities have been permitted to rise into those same ranks, so long as they embraced all the right opinions, engaged in all the right virtue signaling, and shed all but the thinnest cosmetic veneer of whatever ethnic culture they or their immediate ancestors might have had.

The shift in the criteria of exclusion left a fascinating track through the history of popular culture in the United States. As with most such tracks, this one is best followed by way of a specific example. The one I have in mind is a simple musical instrument. It could once be found all over the subculture of the politically avant-garde, but at this point it has been erased from that setting, and the received history of the American Left, as thoroughly as one of Stalin's rivals from a Politburo group photo. The instrument I have in mind is the mountain dulcimer.

Mention the word *dulcimer* nowadays, and dollars will get you doughnuts most of your listeners will think you're talking about the hammered dulcimer, an ancestor of the piano with a long history in various corners of Eurasia. The mountain dulcimer, Appalachian dulcimer, or lap dulcimer—all three terms have been used for it—is not a hammered dulcimer. It's plucked or strummed, not played with hammers; it's got four strings, asymmetrically arranged; it's got a fretboard like a guitar, but with oddly spaced frets—music geeks will recognize it as a diatonic rather than a chromatic fretboard. It's made in various shapes and played in various styles, and it came into being somewhere in the southern end of Appalachia, where half a dozen old European folk instruments may have helped inspire the anonymous craftspeople who originated it a couple of centuries ago.

It's easy to make a dulcimer that sounds good, even if you're dirt poor and your access to raw materials is limited to what you can get in a little village up in the mountains of Kentucky or Georgia, and it's easy to learn how to play it well enough to provide a little additional beauty to the folk songs and Christian hymns that make up most of traditional Appalachian musical culture. That's why the mountain dulcimer became one of the standard folk instruments across the Appalachians, and that, in turn, is why Jean Ritchie learned it as she grew up in the little town of Viper, Kentucky. Later, she left home to get trained in social work, which is how she ended up in New York City, where local beatniks (that's how the word *hipsters* was spelled in those days) were entranced by her dulcimer music.

Folk music, you see, was the music of the avant-garde back then—and no, we're not talking about the folk music of foreign cultures conveniently distant from the gritty realities of American life. If you were young and hip in the 1950s, you listened to *American* folk music. That wasn't the only thing the avant-garde liked to hear, to be sure. Folk music from some other countries, notably Ireland, also got substantial audiences in that demographic. Jazz was another major musical genre there, the more recherché the better—you can still get a reminiscent smile onto the face of people who were there at the time by mentioning Thelonious Monk, Dave Brubeck, et al.—but American folk music was one of the common musical currencies of the alternative scene in those days.

Think about that for a moment: the cultural avant-garde, politically liberal, socially conscious, idealistic . . . listening enthusiastically to the music of the deplorables. Unthinkable as it is today, that was a widespread social reality from the 1950s through the 1970s.

That's the way things were when Jean Ritchie found her dulcimer playing attracting the rapt attention of beatniks in New York City. Of course the inevitable happened; craftspeople with a taste for woodworking started making dulcimers, starry-eyed young people started playing them, and for some decades thereafter, the mountain dulcimer was a minor phenomenon all across the leftward end of society. You could get instructional books from all the folk music publishers, you could buy dulcimers in any well-equipped folk music store, and the drone-and-melody version of "Boil Them Cabbage Down"—traditionally the first tune everyone learns on the dulcimer—could be heard in pretty much every corner of the country.

Of course none of this happened in a vacuum. From the 1950s through the early 1980s, folk culture—honest, handmade, endearingly clunky, and regionally specific—was a major resource for the leftward end of alternative culture. High technology marketed by big corporations? That was the mark of the Establishment, which had about the same connotations in the youth culture of the time that the Mark of the Beast has among rock-ribbed Christian fundamentalists today. A great many people, not all of them young by any means, recognized the downsides of dependence on a profit-centered and environmentally destructive corporate industrial system, and folk crafts, folk music, and folk culture generally were among the resources they used to build an alternative.

I spent a lot of time underfoot in the Pacific Northwest version of that subculture in my teen years. It overlapped to a great extent with the appropriate-technology scene, which was a major interest of mine; unsurprisingly, a lot of people who recognized that modern industrial society was sawing off the branch on which it sat found plenty to learn from regional folk cultures that didn't depend anything like so much on the products of fossil-fueled industry. It also overlapped to nearly as large an extent with the alternative-spirituality scene, which was another major interest of mine; unsurprisingly, a lot of people who were passionately exploring the far reaches of human potential in those days found plenty to value in learning to do and make things for themselves, rather than sucking at the teat of the industrial economy.

What I didn't realize, as I strummed out "Boil Them Cabbage Down" on my first mountain dulcimer, helped build a wind turbine for a little communal farm in Bellingham, Washington, and immersed myself in the daily meditations and abstruse studies of traditional Western occultism, was that the overlapping subcultures that appealed so strongly to me were in their last autumnal days before the coming of a bitter winter. I recall with quite some clarity the day in the mid-1980s that I walked into a folk music store in Seattle to find not a single book of mountain dulcimer music, and a question to the store clerk got the snarled response, "We don't carry that stuff here."

That was when the avant-garde dropped American folk music like a hot rock, and "folk music" thereafter meant the music of folk cultures distant enough from the United States to be wrapped in a warm glow of romantic fantasy. Right around that same time, the periodicals that catered to the avant-garde stopped talking about crafts and folk culture, and started babbling instead about the wonders of the newly hatched internet and the gaudy high-tech future we were all going to get once we stopped asking hard questions about the environment and got with the program. Ronald Reagan was in the White House, it was morning in America, and this nation was on its way into a long vacation from reality.

None of this should have been unexpected. It's not at all uncommon for a rising social movement in American public life to start out embracing American folk culture and end up stuffing it into the first convenient memory hole it could find. Nor is it the first time that the poor and working-class people of the flyover states have found themselves suddenly redefined, by one and the same middle-class cultural sector, from adorable to deplorable.

Go into any library that hasn't done a thorough job of censoring the past via Orwellian purges of its book collection—a fashionable habit these days among library administrators—and you may just find a copy of the Works Project Administration folklore and folk culture handbook for your state. Back in the early days of the New Deal, young idealists fired up by Franklin D. Roosevelt's vision of national unity prowled the backroads of the nation, taking down stories and songs and folk customs. American folk music was a hot cultural property then, too, when Burl Ives was a young man and Woodie Guthrie was still on the right side of the grass. Fast forward twenty years or so, and those same individuals, no longer young and not half so idealistic as they claimed, were cultivating a taste for opera and pretending they'd never so much as seen a guitar. Their children in the Sixties, of course, then followed the same trajectory in turn.

That trajectory has a long history. It happened in the Progressive era; it happened among the Transcendentalists, whose vegetarian, pacifist, long-haired hippie communes circa 1820 gave Nathaniel Hawthorne the raw material for his brilliant novel *The Blithedale Romance;* it happened before the Revolutionary War, when communes sprouted in rural Pennsylvania and Rhode Island was a hotbed of occultism and deviant religion. After the middle-class turn to folk culture comes the turn away from it: the former radicals sell out, settle down, embrace everything they claimed they'd rejected forever, and become clones of the older generation they once affected to despise.

Behind this dynamic is the most enduring of the cultural divides in American society, the chasm between the urban enclaves of the periphery—prosperous, irreligious, and culturally dependent on European models—and the impoverished hinterlands, with their loyalty to Protestant religiosity and American folk culture. That divide came into being long before the Revolutionary War and it's been a massive influence on our culture and politics ever since. What makes this relevant to the present subject is that the peripheral urban enclaves are the seats of institutional power in the United States, while the rural hinterlands are an immense but usually inert source of political power not locked into institutional forms.

Movements for social change that restrict their activities to the urban enclaves get nowhere, because they're confronting the Establishment on its own turf and can easily be coopted or destroyed. It's when a movement for social change makes common ground with the unorganized masses of the heartland that real change becomes a possibility. Once the movement for social change takes power, though, it necessarily focuses its attention on the urban enclaves from which institutional power is exercised. Those movements that unseat the Establishment become the Establishment, and make common cause with the remnants of the Establishment they supplant, while those that are coopted by the Establishment get to the same endpoint in a slightly quicker fashion. "Meet the new boss," the Who sang, "same as the old boss": it's a common phenomenon, in America as elsewhere.

There's more to it than that, of course. Movements for social change do, by and large, enact social change once they take power. The New Dealers of the 1930s and the Boomers of the 1980s, like their older equivalents going back to colonial times, did in fact change things, and some of those changes were both useful and enduring. If the changes ground to a halt once the former radicals settled into positions of wealth and power, and doing favors for their rich pals eventually took the place of anything more constructive, that's the ordinary rhythm of change in a democratic society—a real democracy, that is, where people are free to be as stupid and greedy as they wish at the ballot box—and can be traced straight back through history to the oldest democratic societies on record.

The rise and fall of folk culture in twentieth-century American public life is simply one of many reflections of this well-rehearsed dynamic. In the 1950s and 1960s, the social and generational cohorts that now occupy the seats of power in the United States were young, still relatively idealistic, and eager for power, so they turned—as young, idealistic, power-hungry Americans have always turned—to the great reservoir of untapped political strength in the hinterlands, to counterbalance the institutional power of the peripheral urban Establishment. The Boomer generation was just a little quicker to cash in its ideals than most of its equivalents, and the resulting 180-degree turn gave those of us who didn't take the bait a bad case of mental whiplash at the time.

Still, the logic was simple enough. Having sold out to the Establishment, they no longer wanted to encourage anyone else to rebel against it. Rather, the goal of cultural activity in the avant-garde once the transaction had taken place was what it always is in an aristocracy—that is, shutting out the rabble: in less colorful language, building barriers that the aristocrats can use to exclude others informally from access to the levers of influence and wealth.

The quest for ways to shut out the rabble has had immense impacts on culture in the United States, and not just through the endless parade of virtue signals that are actually, as such things always are, signals of social status. Consider the way that painters, sculptors, composers, and other producers of fine arts in America devoted the entire twentieth century to a heroic effort to drive away the large audiences their equivalents had in 1900. Back then a gallery opening or the premiere of a new opera attracted the enthusiastic attention and patronage of the general public, and artists deliberately courted success along those lines. Giuseppe Verdi, one of the two supreme opera composers of the late nineteenth century, earnestly advised the man who became the general manager of the Metropolitan Opera in New York to ignore the critics and pay close attention to box-office receipts instead.

What happened? In America, at least, the fine arts became a means of exclusion by which the aristocracy distinguished itself from the rabble. Paintings that anybody could appreciate became the kiss of death for anyone who aspired to a career in the fine arts; what brought the prestigious shows and the financial rewards were *objets d'art* that looked like a dog's breakfast the second time around, because no one outside the circles of the elite even pretended to like them. In the same way, young composers were taught to avoid writing anything an audience might enjoy listening to: no melody, no tonality, nothing that would appeal to anybody outside the narrowing circle of the cognoscenti. We can't have the rabble enjoying *our* music!

During the twentieth century, maneuvers of this kind ensured that only the privileged classes and their hangers-on paid any attention to the fine arts, and so allowed the privileged to use Andy Warhol's artworks, John Cage's music, and other products of the same kind as caste markers and signals of their status. At this point, however, the quest to drive off the audience has reached such a pitch in art schools, conservatories, and the like that it's succeeded in driving off most of the privileged classes as well. Painters, composers, and the like are creating works these days solely for each other and a tiny audience that mostly belongs to the academic scene. We'll probably have to wait until the student loan bubble pops, and takes most of U.S. higher education with it, before artists remember that art is an act of communication, not of exclusion, and that it's their job to reach out to their audience—not the audience's job to struggle to wrestle some drop or other of meaning out of an opaque and unappealing product.

✳

The same class divisions we've just traced, and the habits of exclusion used to enforce them, played a central role in the destruction of the American wage class. All along, there was a straightforward solution to the bitter economic troubles that overwhelmed the wage class during the fifty years from 1966 to 2016, and most members of the wage class were perfectly able to explain exactly what that was: a change in government policies that would provide enough full-time jobs at decent wages to give them the chance to lift their families out of poverty.

The reason why tens of thousands of American communities plunged into poverty and misery during those years was that too few people had enough income to support the small businesses and local economies that used to thrive there. The money that used to keep main streets bustling across the United States, the wages that used to be paid on Friday afternoons to millions of Americans who'd spent the previous week putting in an honest day's work for an honest day's pay, had been choked off by half a century of government policies that benefited the salary class disproportionately at the expense of the wage class.

Until 2016, however, the impact of those policies on the wage class was effectively shut out of discussions in the public sphere. To some extent, that was defended by way of sustained efforts by both of the major U.S. parties to lure wage-class voters into backing candidates on grounds unrelated to their economic interests. In both cases, as so often before in American history, rhetorics of moral virtue formed the centerpiece of these efforts at distraction. The language of conservative Christian morals played the same role for Republicans that the language of social justice played for the Democrats. It was effective magic so long as all sides adhered to it. Wage-class voters, frustrated that the issues that mattered most to them received only lip service, still lined up without enthusiasm to vote for the party that offended them least.

Far more important as a means of exclusion, though, was the response of the salary class to any attempt by members of the wage class to bring up the issues that mattered to them. On the rare occasions when that happened in the public sphere, the spokespeople of the wage class got shouted down with a degree of venom hard to square with the standard salary-class posture of enlightened tolerance. The same tune gets played in a different mode in less public settings. If you doubt this—and you probably do, if you belong to the salary class—try this experiment: get a bunch of your salary-class friends together in some casual context and start them talking about ordinary American working guys. What you'll hear will range from crude caricatures and one-dimensional stereotypes right on up to bona fide hate speech.

People in the wage class are aware of this. They've heard it all, over and over again. They're used to being called stupid, ignorant, and so on, ad nauseam, for failing to agree with whatever item of self-serving dogma some representative of the salary class tries to push on them. The result is that nowadays, when wage-class Americans get addressed by the salary class, their default assumption is that the salary class is lying.

What's more, they have very good reasons for thinking this. The talking heads insisted that handing over tax dollars to huge corporation would bring jobs back to American communities; the corporations in question pocketed the tax dollars and walked away. The talking heads insisted that if working-class people went to college at their own expense and got retrained in new skills, that would bring jobs back to American communities; universities and banks profited mightily but the jobs never showed up, leaving millions of people so deeply in debt that most of them will never recover financially. The talking heads insisted that this or that or the other political candidate would bring jobs back to American communities by pursuing the same policies that got rid of the jobs in the first place, and we know how that turned out.

The same loss of faith can be traced in plenty of other dimensions of American life these days. Consider the way that herbal medicine—"God's medicine" is the usual phrase these days—has supplanted modern medicine among a huge number of devout wage-class Christians. There are plenty of reasons why that should be happening, but surely one of the most crucial is the loss of faith in the salary-class talking heads that sell modern medicine to consumers. Here again, that loss of faith is grounded in hard experience. Herbs may not be as effective as modern pharmaceuticals in treating major illnesses, but they rarely have the ghastly side effects that so many pharmaceuticals will give you. Just as crucially, nobody ever went bankrupt and ended up on the street because of the high price of herbs.

The collapse of trust in the salary class turned into a major barrier to Hillary Clinton's presidential ambitions. It also frustrated the attempts by the media during the campaign to pin various negative labels on Trump. Those backfired consistently, since the wage-class voters that Clinton needed to win over assumed as a matter of course that she and the media were lying to them. It's only fair to say that Clinton's campaign and the mainstream U.S. media both gave them plenty of help in reaching this conclusion. On the one hand, Clinton's speeches and campaign literature seem to have been drawn up on the premise that promising more benefits to the salary class and piling more burdens on the wage class would convince the latter to vote for her. On the other, the corporate media in the United States seemed unable to get past the odd conviction that people in the flyover states would be shocked and horrified to learn that Trump had done something to upset the feelings of well-to-do coastal liberals.

The absurdity reached fever pitch when salary-class pundits published agitated papers insisting that Trump supporters had to be suffering from some strange psychological condition, because exposure to a propaganda video meant to convince them not to vote for him had the opposite effect. As far as I know, the possibility that wage-class voters might have seen enough salary-class propaganda to discount it automatically never entered the discussion. It was all very reminiscent of the talk in the antebellum South about "drapetomania"— a strange mental condition that, so it was claimed, caused slaves to run away from their masters for no reason at all. The slaves, like the wage-class voters, could readily have enlightened the pundits as to what was actually going on, but the viewpoints of those whose actions were being judged weren't welcome in either discussion.

Behind the absurdity, though, lies a deep and troubling shift. It used to be, not all that long ago, that ordinary working people in the United States trusted implicitly in American institutions. They were just as prone as any urban sophisticate to distrust this or that politician or businessperson or cultural figure, to be sure. Back in the days when local caucuses and county conventions still counted for something, you could be sure of hearing raucous debates about a galaxy of personalities and issues. Next to nobody in the wage class, though, doubted that the basic structures of American society were not merely sound, but superior to all others.

In the years leading up to 2016, when you heard such claims made at all, they were phrased in the kind of angry and defensive terms that lets everyone know that the speaker is trying to convince himself of something he doesn't entirely believe any more, or the kind of elegiac tones that hearken back to an earlier time when things still seemed to work—when the phrase "the American Dream" still stood for a reality that many people had experienced and many more could expect to achieve for themselves and their children. It became common to regard the U.S. federal government as a vast mechanism operated by rich crooks for their own benefit, at the expense of everyone else. What's more, the same cynical attitude spread to embrace the other institutions of American society, and—lethally—the ideals from which those institutions get whatever legitimacy they still hold in the eyes of the people.

Those readers who recall the late 1980s and early 1990s have seen this movie before, though it came with Cyrillic subtitles then. By 1985 or so, it had become painfully obvious to most citizens of the Soviet Union that the grand promises of Marxism would not be kept and the glorious future for which their grandparents and great-grandparents had fought and labored was never going to arrive. Glowing articles in

Pravda and *Izvestia* insisted that everything was fine in the Worker's Paradise; annual five-year plans presupposed that economic conditions would get steadily better, while for most people economic conditions got steadily worse; vast May Day parades showed off the Soviet Union's military might, Soyuz spacecraft circled the globe to display its technological prowess, and tame intellectuals in affluent districts of Moscow and Leningrad, looking forward to their next vacation at their favorite Black Sea resort, chattered in print about the good life under socialism, while millions of ordinary Soviet citizens trudged through a bleak round of long lines, product shortages, and system-wide dysfunction. Then crisis hit, and the great-great-grandchildren of the people who surged to the barricades during the Russian Revolution shrugged, and let the Soviet Union unravel in a matter of days.

We are much closer to a similar cascade of events here in the United States than most people realize. Dmitry Orlov pointed out years back in his book *Reinventing Collapse* that the differences between the Soviet Union and the United States were far less important than their similarities, and that a Soviet-style collapse was a real possibility here—a possibility for which most Americans were far less well prepared than their Russian equivalents in the early 1990s. His arguments have become even more compelling as the years have passed, and the United States has become mired ever more deeply in a mire of institutional dysfunction and politico-economic kleptocracy all but indistinguishable from the one that swallowed its erstwhile rival.

During the Obama years, the parallels stood out with savage clarity. We had news articles insisting, in tones by turns glowing and shrill, that things have never been better in the United States and anyone who said otherwise was just plain wrong; we had economic pronouncements predicated on continuing growth at a time when economic growth in the United States was a statistical fiction propped up by unsustainable debt levels; we had overblown displays of military might and technological prowess, reminiscent of nothing so much as the macho posturing of balding middle-aged former athletes who are trying to pretend that they haven't lost it; we had tame intellectuals comfortably situated in affluent suburban districts around Boston, New York, Washington, and San Francisco, looking forward to their next vacation in whatever the currently fashionable spot happened to be, babbling on the internet about the good life under predatory cybercapitalism. Meanwhile millions of Americans trudged through a bleak round of layoffs, wage cuts, part-time jobs at minimal pay, and system-wide dysfunction.

The one significant difference between the Soviet trajectory and its American echo is that Soviet citizens had no choice but to accept the leaders the Communist Party of the USSR foisted off on them, from Brezhnev to Andropov to Chernenko to Gorbachev, until the system collapsed of its own weight. American citizens, by contrast, had a choice. Elections in the United States have been riddled with fraud throughout our nation's history, but since both parties engage in ballot rigging to a roughly equal degree, fraud mostly swings close elections. It's still possible for a sufficiently popular candidate to overwhelm the graveyard vote, the crooked voting machines, and the other crass realities of American elections by sheer force of numbers, and elbow his way into the White House—and that was what happened in 2016.

3

The Pallid Mask

Spells of Privilege, Prejudice, and Injustice

"The ambition of Caesar and of Napoleon pales before that which could not rest until it had seized the minds of men and controlled even their unborn thoughts," said Mr. Wilde.

"You are speaking of the King in Yellow," I groaned, with a shudder.

FROM "THE REPAIRER OF REPUTATIONS"

IN *THE KING IN YELLOW*

Of course this is not how the 2016 election has been defined by those who were outraged by its results. Ioan Couliano analysis of today's industrial societies function as "magician states," is especially trenchant in this context. In today's United States, as a result of the sorceries of the media, certain obvious and highly significant dimensions of class interest and class prejudice are among the things that have been erased from public discourse, and so the populist insurgency that put Trump into the White House has had to be redefined in a way that supported the interests and the prejudices of the salary class.

Thus it quickly became articles of faith among Democrats, as already noted, that those who voted for Donald Trump could only have done so because of racism, sexism, or some other set of attitudes most Americans these days consider offensive, and that the Trump campaign had somehow rigged the election with the aid of sinister Russian agents of influence. Those claims were not true. Anyone who took the time to listen to Trump's voters could find out readily that the first claim was not true, and repeated investigations trying to find dirt on Trump unwittingly showed that the second was just as false. Yet the same mechanisms of exclusion discussed in the previous chapter found ample employment in silencing discussion of the actual reasons Trump was elected—above all else, the politics of social class and the economic consequences of the policies that the salary class supported.

Words like *racism* and *sexism* deserve a closer look here, though. These and terms like them are much more ambiguous than they look at first glance. Each such term conflates at least three different things. Unpacking those here will help us get a clearer view of the landscape of American inequality, and its impact on the rise of Donald Trump.

The distinct factors that need to be pulled out of these portmanteau words are *privilege, prejudice,* and *injustice.* Let's start with the last. A policeman guns down a black teenager in response to an action that would not have gotten a white teenager shot; a woman who is raped has a much lower chance of having police and prosecutors bring the case to trial than a man who suffers an assault; until quite recently, two people who loved each other and wanted to get married had to run a gauntlet of difficulties if they happened to be the same sex that they would not have faced if they were of different sexes. Those are acts of injustice.

Prejudice is a matter of attitudes rather than actions. The word literally means pre-judgments, the judgments we all make about people and situations before we encounter them. Everybody has them, every culture teaches them, but some people are more prejudiced—more committed to their pre-judgments, and less willing to reassess them in the face of disconfirming evidence—and some are less so. Acts of injustice are often motivated by prejudice, and prejudice often results in acts of injustice, but neither of these equations is exact. I've known people who were profoundly prejudiced but refused to act on their prejudices because some other belief or commitment forbade that. I've also known people who participated repeatedly in acts of injustice, who were just following orders or going along with friends, and didn't care in the least one way or the other.

Then there's privilege. Where prejudice and acts of injustice are individual, privilege is collective. You have privilege, or don't have it, because of the categories you belong to, not because of what you do or don't do. I'll use myself as a source of examples here. I can walk through well-to-do neighborhoods, for instance, without being hassled by the police; black people by and large don't have that privilege. I can publish controversial essays online without being bombarded with rape and death threats by internet trolls; women by and large don't have that privilege. I can kiss my spouse in public without having some moron yell insults at me out of the window of a passing car; gay people by and large don't have that privilege.

I could fill the next half dozen pages with a listing of similar privileges I have, and not come close to running out of examples. It's important, though, to recognize that my condition of privilege isn't assigned to me for any one reason. It's not just that I'm white, or male, or heterosexual, or grew up in a family on the bottom end of the salary class, or was born and remain able-bodied, or what have you. It's all of these things and many more, taken together, that assign me my place in the hierarchy of privilege. This is equally true of you, dear reader, and of everyone else. What differentiates my position from yours, and yours from everyone else's, is that every station on the ladder has a different proportion between the number of people above it and the number below. There are, for example, plenty of people in today's America who have more privilege than I do, but there are vastly more who have much, much less.

Note also that I don't have to do anything to get the privileges I have, nor can I get rid of them. As a white heterosexual man from a salary-class background, and the rest of it, I got assigned nearly all of my privileges the moment I was born, and no matter what I do or don't do, I'll keep the vast majority of them until I die. This is also true of you, dear reader, and of everyone else. The vast majority of what places you on whatever rung you occupy in the long ladder of privilege is yours simply for being born. Thus you're not responsible for the fact that you have whatever level of privilege you do—though you are responsible, of course, for what you choose to do with it.

You can, after all, convince yourself that you deserve your privilege, and that less privileged people deserve their inferior status—that is to say, you can choose to be prejudiced. You can exploit your privilege to benefit yourself at the expense of the less privileged—that is to say, you can engage in acts of injustice. The more privilege you have, the more your prejudices affect other people's lives and the more powerful your acts of injustice become. Thus advocates for the less privileged are quite correct to point out that the prejudices and injustices of those who have more privilege matter more than comparable acts by those who have less.

On the other hand, privilege does not automatically equate to prejudice, or to acts of injustice. It's possible for the privileged—who, as already noted, did not choose their privilege and can't get rid of it—to refuse to exploit their privilege in this way. It's possible, crashingly unfashionable as the concept is these days, for them to take up the old principle of *noblesse oblige:* the concept, widely accepted in eras where privilege was openly recognized, that those who are born to privilege also inherit definite responsibilities toward the less privileged. I suppose it's even possible that they might do this and not expect lavish praise for it, though that's kind of a stretch, American culture today being what it is.

These days, though, most white heterosexual men from salary-class backgrounds don't think of themselves as privileged, and don't see the things I enumerated earlier as privileges. This is one of the most crucial points about privilege in today's America: *to the privileged, privilege is invisible.* That's not just a matter of personal cluelessness or of personal isolation from the less privileged, though these can of course be involved. It's one of the most significant magical spells we're under. The mass media and every other aspect of mainstream American culture constantly present the experience of privileged people as normal, and just as constantly feed any departure from that experience through an utterly predictable set of filters.

First, of course, the experience of the less privileged is erased—"That sort of thing doesn't actually happen." When that fails, it's dismissed as unimportant—"Well, maybe it does happen, but it's no big deal." When it becomes clear that it is a big deal to those who have to cope with it, it's treated as an occasional anomaly—"You can't generalize from one or two bad examples." When that breaks down, finally, the experience of the less privileged is blamed on the less privileged—"It's their own fault that they get treated like that." If you know your way around America's collective nonconversation about privilege, in the mass media or in everyday conversation, you've seen each one of these filters deployed a thousand times or more.

What makes this interesting is that the invisibility of privilege in modern America isn't shared by that many other human societies. There are many more cultures, past and present, in which privilege is right out there in the open, written into laws, and openly discussed by the privileged as well as the unprivileged. The United States used to be like that as recently as the 1950s. It wasn't just that there were Jim Crow laws in those days formally assigning black Americans the status of second-class citizens, and laws in many states that gave women second-class status when it came to a galaxy of legal and financial rights; it was all over the media and popular culture, too. Open any daily newspaper back then, and the society pages detailed the difference in privilege between those people who belonged to the elite and those who didn't.

For reasons rooted in the cultural convulsions of the Sixties, though, frank talk about privilege stopped being socially acceptable in America over the course of the second half of the twentieth century. That didn't make privilege go away, of course. It did mean that some specific forms of privilege based on race and gender, such as the Jim Crow laws just mentioned, were scrapped, and in that process, some real injustices did get fixed. The downside was the rise of a culture of doubletalk in which frank talk about class privilege and class prejudice—above all, about the privilege enjoyed by members of the salary class and the prejudices they displayed toward the wage class—was shoved completely out of the collective conversation of our time.

That act of suppression had a profoundly political subtext. In the aftermath of the Sixties, the wealthy elite, occupying core positions of power in the United States, offered a tacit bargain to politically active members of the dulcimer-playing generation discussed earlier. Individuals and groups who were willing to give up the struggle to change the system, and settled instead for an improved place within it, suddenly started to receive corporate and government funding, and carefully vetted leaders from within the movements in question were brought into elite circles as junior partners. Those individuals and groups who refused these blandishments were marginalized, generally with the help of their more compliant peers.

If you've ever wondered why environmental groups such as the Sierra Club and Friends of the Earth changed so quickly from scruffy fire-breathing activists to slick, well-funded corporate enablers, this is why. Equally, that's why mainstream feminist organizations by and large stopped worrying about the concerns of the great majority of women and fixated instead on "breaking the glass ceiling"—that is to say, giving women who belong to the salary and investment classes access to more privilege than they have already. The core demand placed on former radicals who wanted to cash in on the offer, though, was that they drop their demands for economic justice—and American society being what it is, that meant that they had to stop talking about class issues altogether.

A good many American radicals were already willing to meet them halfway. The New Left of the 1960s, like the old Left of the between-the-wars era, was mostly Marxist in its theoretical underpinnings, and so was hamstrung by the mismatch between Marxist theory and one of the enduring realities of American politics. According to Marxist theory, socialist revolution is led by the radicalized salary-class intelligentsia, but it gets the muscle it needs to overthrow the capitalist system from the wage class. This is the rock on which wave after wave of American Marxist activism has broken and gone streaming back out to sea, because the American wage class has always been serenely uninterested in taking up the world-historical role that Marxist theory assigns to them. What most of its members want is plenty of full time jobs at a living wage. Give them that, and revolutionary activists can bellow themselves hoarse without getting the least flicker of interest out of them.

Every so often, the investment and salary classes lose track of this, and try to force the wage class to put up with extensive joblessness and low pay, so that more affluent Americans can pocket the proceeds. This never ends well. After an interval, the wage class picks up whatever blunt instrument is handy—Andrew Jackson, the Grange, the Populist Party, the New Deal, Donald Trump—and beats the more affluent classes about the head and shoulders with it until the latter finally get a clue. This might seem promising for Marxist revolutionaries. It isn't, because the Marxist revolutionaries inevitably rush in saying, in effect, "No, no, you shouldn't settle for plenty of full-time jobs at a living wage; you should die by the tens of thousands in an orgy of revolutionary violence so that we can seize power in your name." My readers are welcome to imagine the response of ordinary American working people to this suggestion.

The New Left, like the other American Marxist movements before its time, thus had a bruising face-first collision with cognitive dissonance. Its supposedly infallible theory said one thing, but the facts refused to play along and said something very different. For much of the Sixties and Seventies, New Left theoreticians tried to cope with this by coming up with increasingly Byzantine redefinitions of "working class" that excluded the actual working class, so that they could continue to believe devoutly in the inevitability and imminence of the proletarian revolution that the prophecies of Marx promised them. Around the time that this effort finally petered out into absurdity, it was replaced by the core concept of the identity politics currently central to the American Left, which I introduced a chapter ago: the conviction that the only divisions in American society that matter are those that have some basis in biology.

Skin color, gender, ethnicity, sexual orientation, disability—these are the divisions that the American Left likes to talk about, to the exclusion of all other social divisions, and especially to the exclusion of social class. Are the divisions listed above important when it comes to discriminatory treatment in America today? Of course they are—*but social class is also important.* It's by way of the erasure of social class as a major factor in American injustice that we wind up in the absurd situation in which a woman of color who makes a quarter million dollars a year plus benefits as a New York stockbroker can claim to be oppressed by a white guy in Indiana who's working three part-time jobs at minimum wage with no benefits in a desperate effort to keep his kids fed, when the political candidates that she supports and the economic policies from which she profits are directly responsible for his plight.

Thus it's a source of repeated amusement to me that members of the salary class in this country so often inveigh against the horrors of class warfare. Class warfare is their bread and butter. The ongoing warfare of the salary class against the wage class is a core factor in creating and maintaining the disparities of wealth and privilege in contemporary American society. What upsets the salary class about class warfare is simply the fear that they might someday be treated the way they treat those below them.

That, in turn, is a massive part of the reason Trump's presidency is so unacceptable to so many affluent Americans: his adminstration, unlike those of all his rivals, was primarily backed by *"those* people"— that is, by the wage class. (I'm old enough to remember when the words *"those* people," spoken by middle- and upper middle-class white people with exactly the same tone of voice and curled lip, invariably meant people of color; the fact that it now means white working-class people is a useful testimony to the way that class bigotry has supplanted racial bigotry as the prejudice du jour among our privileged classes.)

A great deal of effort has gone into obfuscating that point in order to drag the discussion back to some less threatening set of categories. Here Couliano's discussion of "magician states" is particularly relevant, because the methods used in the attempt to stave off discussion of class issues in today's America are best described as incantations. During the run-up to the 2016 election, and even more so afterward, talking heads in the mainstream U.S. media seemed unable to utter the words "working class" without sticking the labels "white" in front and "men" behind. The resulting rhetoric implied, and occasionally stated, that the minority of the American voting public that happens to be white, male, and deplorable somehow managed to hand the election to Donald Trump all by itself, despite the united efforts of everyone else.

Of course that's not what happened. A substantial majority of white women also voted for Trump in 2016 and 2020, for example. So, according to exit polls, did men and women of color—a moderate number of them in 2016, and a very large and politically revolutionary number of them four years later. Add it all up, and you'll find that the majority of people who voted for Trump each time weren't white working-class men at all—and then there was the huge number of registered voters of all races and genders who usually turn out for Democratic candidates, but stayed home in disgust in 2016 and deprived Clinton of the turnout that could have given her the victory.

Somehow, though, pundits and activists who fly to their keyboards at a moment's notice to denounce the erasure of women and people of color in any other context eagerly cooperated in the erasure of women and people of color in this one case. What's more, that same erasure began as soon as the 2016 campaign started and has continued ever since. (How much discussion have you seen in the corporate media of the political opinions of working-class women, or working-class people of color?) Those of my readers who followed the media coverage of both campaigns will recall the repeated claims that women wouldn't vote for

Trump because his words and actions had given offense to certain feminists, that Hispanics (or people of color in general) wouldn't vote for Trump because social-justice activists denounced his attitudes toward illegal immigrants from Mexico as racist, and so on. The media took these incantations as simple statements of fact—and of course that was one of the reasons the media was blindsided by Trump's victory.

The facts of the matter are that a great many American women, especially but not only in the wage class, don't happen to agree with salary-class feminists, nor do all people of color agree with the salary-class, social-justice activists who claim to speak in their name. For that matter, it's frankly embarrassing how much of the United States mainstream media acts as though the terms "Hispanic" and "Mexican-American" are synonyms. Americans of Hispanic descent trace their ancestry to many different nations of origin, each of which has its own distinctive culture and history, and treating them as a single monolithic electoral bloc is not merely mistaken but—yes, the word that comes to mind is "racist." (The Cuban-American community in Florida, to cite only one of the more obvious examples, votes Republican far more often than not, and played a significant role in giving that electoral vote-rich state to Trump in both elections.)

Behind the media's portrayal of white working-class men as the cackling villains who gave the country to Donald Trump, in other words, lies a reality far more in keeping with the complexities of American electoral politics: a ramshackle coalition of many different voting blocs and interest groups, each with an assortment of reasons for voting for a candidate who was feared and despised by the U.S. political establishment and its tame media. That coalition included a very large majority of the U.S. wage class. While white wage-class voters of both genders were disproportionately more likely to have voted for Trump than working-class people of color, it wasn't simply a matter of whiteness, or for that matter maleness.

It was, however, to a very great extent a matter of social class. This isn't just because so large a fraction of wage-class voters generally backed

Trump; it's also because Trump saw this from the beginning, and aimed his campaign squarely at the wage-class vote. His signature red ball cap was part of that—can you imagine Hillary Clinton wearing so proletarian a garment without absurdity?—but so was his deliberate strategy of saying (and tweeting) things that would get the liberal punditocracy to denounce him. The tones of contempt and condescension they directed at him were all too familiar to his wage-class audiences, who have been treated to the same tones unceasingly by their self-proclaimed betters for decades now.

To go deeper, and make sense of the way that the unmentionable realities of social class have shaped and distorted the political imagination of our time, it's going to be necessary to try to make an unfamiliar kind of sense of the narratives commonly used to frame discussions about privilege, prejudice, and acts of injustice in the United States today. It's crucial to keep in mind that this discussion is about narratives, not about the things that the narratives are supposed to describe. If you want to hear about the realities of racial privilege, racial prejudice, and racial injustice in the United States, you need to talk to the people of color who have to deal with those things day in and day out, not to a middle-aged white intellectual like me, who's been sheltered from many aspects of that dimension of the American experience.

People of color, on the other hand, have had very little influence on the officially approved narratives of race in the United States. Like most of the narratives that shape our collective discourse, the narratives of race have been crafted primarily by middle-aged white intellectuals with college educations and salary-class backgrounds: that is, people like me. If I sing you one of the songs of my people, in other words, I hope you won't mind.

Once again I'm going to approach the opening notes of this song by what may seem like a roundabout route. There's a school of psychology called "transactional analysis," which focuses on interactions between people rather than the vagaries of the individual psyche. Transactional analysis covers a lot of ground, but I want to focus on just one of its themes here: the theory of interpersonal games.

An interpersonal game, like most other games, has a set of rules and some kind of prizes for winners. In a healthy interpersonal game, the rules and the prizes are overt: that is, if you ask the players what the rules and prizes are, you can pretty much count on an honest answer. As this stops being true—as more of the rules and prizes become covert—the game becomes more and more dysfunctional. At the far end of the spectrum are those wholly dysfunctional games in which straight talk about the rules and payoffs is utterly taboo.

The accepted mainstream narratives about privilege, prejudice, and acts of injustice in America today can best be described as one of those latter category of wholly dysfunctional games. Fortunately, it's a game that was explored in quite a bit of detail by transactional analysts in the 1960s and 1970s, so it won't be particularly difficult to break the taboo and speak about the unspeakable. It has been given several names in the literature; the one I encountered first, and still find most evocative, is the Rescue Game.

Here's how it works. Each group of players is assigned one of three roles: Victim, Persecutor, or Rescuer. The first two roles are allowed one move each: the Victim's move is to suffer, and the Persecutor's move is to make the Victim suffer. The Rescuer is allowed two moves: to sympathize with the Victim and to punish the Persecutor. No other moves are allowed, and no player is allowed to make a move that belongs to a different role.

That may seem unduly limited. It's not, because when a group of people is assigned a role, all their actions are redefined as the move or moves allotted to that role. In the Rescue Game, in other words, whatever a Victim does must be interpreted as a cry of pain. Whatever a Persecutor does is treated as something that's intended to cause pain to a Victim, and whatever a Rescuer does, by definition, either expresses sympathy for a Victim or inflicts well-deserved punishment on a Persecutor. This is true even when the actions performed by the three people in question happen to be identical. In a well-played Rescue Game, quite a bit of ingenuity can go into assigning every action its proper meaning as a move.

What's more, the roles are collective, not individual. Each Victim is equal to every other Victim, and is expected to feel and resent all the suffering ever inflicted on every other Victim in the same game. Each Persecutor is equal to every other Persecutor, and so is personally to blame for every suffering inflicted by every other Persecutor in the same game. Each Rescuer, in turn, is equal to every other Rescuer, and so may take personal credit for the actions of every other Rescuer in the same game. This allows the range of potential moves to expand to infinity without ever leaving the narrow confines of the game.

There's one other rule: the game must go on forever. The Victim must continue to suffer, the Persecutor must continue to persecute, and the Rescuer must continue to sympathize and punish. Anything that might end the game—for example, any change in the condition of the Victim or the behavior of the Persecutor—is therefore out of bounds. The Rescuer also functions as a referee, and so it's primarily his or her job to see that nothing gets in the way of the continuation of the game, but all players are expected to help out if that should be necessary.

Got it? Now we'll go to an example—and no, it's not the one you're probably thinking of. The example I have in mind is the standard narrative of race in the Deep South for the century or so after the Civil War. The players were rich white people, poor white people, and black people—this latter category, in the jargon of the time, included anyone with any publicly acknowledged trace of African ancestry. The roles were assigned as follows: poor white people were Victims, black people were Persecutors, and rich white people were Rescuers. The rest of the game followed from there.

Anything that poor white people did to black people was thus justified, under the rules of the game, as a cry of pain elicited by their suffering at the hands of Yankees, carpetbaggers, former slaves, and so on.

Anything rich white people did to black people was justified as punishment for the Persecutors or solace for the Victims. Meanwhile, anything and everything that was done, or not done, by black people was defined as a persecution—if black people pursued an education, for example, they were trying to steal jobs from white folk, while if they didn't, that just proved that they were an inferior element corrupting the South by their very presence, and so on through all the classic double binds of bigotry.

A variant of that game still goes on in the pseudoconservative end of American politics. When Hillary Clinton went out of her way to characterize African American youth as "super predators" not that many years ago, she was playing that same game, with law-abiding white citizens as the Victims, black youth as the Persecutors, and white politicians as the Rescuers. On the other end of the political spectrum, of course, the roles are reversed; in games played on that field, people of color are the Victims, working-class white people are the Persecutors, and affluent white liberals are the Rescuers. The players have changed places but the game's otherwise identical.

A few comments are doubtless necessary before we go further. Yes, I'm aware that people of color on the one hand, and working-class white people on the other, occupy different places in the hierarchy of privilege in today's America. More precisely, members of each of these heterogeneous groups occupy a range of different positions in that hierarchy, and these two ranges have only modest overlaps. What's come to be called intersectionality—the way that social divisions according to gender, race, class, ethnicity, physical disability, and a bubbling cauldron of other factors, intersect with one another to produce the convoluted landscape of American inequality—is a massive factor all through contemporary life in the United States. So is the wretchedly common human habit of "paying it downwards," in which an abused and exploited group responds by seeking some other group to abuse and exploit in turn.

All these considerations, though, belong to the real world. They are excluded from the artificial world of the Rescue Game, and from the official narrative about race that derives from that game. In the Rescue Game, all members of the group assigned the role of Victim are always, only, and equally Victims; all members of the group assigned the role of Persecutor are always, only, and equally Persecutors, and the maltreatment of the Victims by the Persecutors is the only thing that matters. If anyone tries to bring anyone else's treatment of anyone else into the game, it's either dismissed as an irrelevance or denounced as a deliberate, malicious attempt to distract attention from the maltreatment of the Victims by the Persecutors.

The assignment of roles to different categories of people takes place in the opening phase of the Rescue Game. Like most games, this one has an opening phase, a middle period of play, and an endgame, and the opening phase is called "Pin the Tail on the Persecutor." In this initial phase, teams of Victims bid for the attention of Rescuers by displaying their suffering and denouncing their Persecutors, and the winners are those who attract enough Rescuers to make up a full team. In today's America, this phase of the game is ongoing, and a great deal of rivalry tends to spring up between teams of Victims who compete for the attention of the same Rescuers. When that rivalry breaks out into open hostilities, as it often does, the result has been called the Oppression Olympics—the bare-knuckle, no-holds-barred struggle over which group of people gets to have its sufferings privileged over everyone else's.

Once the roles have been assigned and an adequate team of Rescuers attracted, the game moves into its central phase, which is called "Show Trial." This has two requirements, which are not always met. The first is an audience willing to applaud the Victims, shout catcalls at the Persecutors, and cheer for the Rescuers on cue. The second is a supply of Persecutors who can be convinced or coerced into showing up to play the game. A Rescue Game in which the Persecutors don't show quickly enters the endgame, with disadvantages that will be described shortly, and so getting the Persecutors to appear is crucial.

This can be done in several ways. If the game is being played with live ammunition—for example, Stalin's Russia or the Deep South after the Civil War—people who have been assigned the role of Persecutors can simply be rounded up at gunpoint and forced to participate. If the people playing the game have some less drastic form of institutional power—for example, in American universities today—participation in the game can be enforced by incentives such as curriculum requirements. Lacking these options, the usual strategies these days are to invite the Persecutors to a supposedly honest dialogue, on the one hand, and to taunt them until they show up to defend themselves, on the other.

However their presence is arranged, once the Persecutors arrive, the action of the game is stereotyped. The Victims accuse the Persecutors of maltreating them, the Persecutors try to defend themselves, and then the Victims and the Rescuers get to bully the Persecutors into silence, using whatever means are allowed by local law and custom. If the game is being played with live ammunition, each round ends with the messy death of one or more Persecutors, the surviving players take a break of varying length, and then the next Persecutor or group of Persecutors is brought in. In less gory forms of the game, the Persecutors are shouted down rather than shot down, but the emotional tone is much the same.

This phase of the game continues until there are no more Persecutors willing or able to act out their assigned role, or the audience gets bored and wanders away. At this point the action shifts to the end-game, which is called "Circular Firing Squad." In this final phase, the need for a steady supply of Persecutors is met by identifying individual Victims or Rescuers as covert Persecutors. Since players thus accused usually try to defend themselves against the accusation, the game can go on as before—the Victims bring their accusations, the newly identified Persecutors defend themselves, and then the Victims and Rescuers get to bully them into silence.

The one difficulty with this phase is that each round of the game diminishes the supply of players and makes continuing the game harder and harder. Toward the end, in order to keep the game going, the players commonly make heroic attempts to convince or coerce more people into joining the game, so that they can be "outed" as Persecutors, and the range of things used to identify covert Persecutors can become impressively baroque. The difficulty, of course, is that very few people are interested in playing a game in which the only role open to them is that of being accused of violating a code of rules that becomes steadily more subtle, elaborate, and covert with each round of the game, so that they can be bullied into silence. Once word gets out, as a result, the game usually grinds to a halt in short order due to a shortage of players. At that point, it's back to "Pin the Tail on the Persecutor," and on we go.

There's plenty more that could be said here about the details of the Rescue Game and the narrative of race derived from it, but at this point I'd like to consider three broader issues. The first is the relation between the game and the narrative, on the one hand, and the realities of racism in today's America. I don't doubt that some readers of this chapter will insist that by questioning the narrative, I'm trying to erase the reality. Not so. Racial privilege, racial prejudice, and racial injustice are pervasive factors in American life today. The fact that the approved narrative of race in today's America is deceptive and dysfunctional doesn't make racism any less real. On the other hand, the fact that American racism is a reality doesn't make the narrative any less deceptive and dysfunctional.

The second issue I'd like to consider is whether the same game is played on other playing fields, and the answer is yes. I first encountered the concept of the Rescue Game, in fact, by way of a pamphlet lent to my wife many years ago by her therapist sister-in-law, which used transactional analysis as the basis for an edgy analysis of class conflicts within the lesbian community. From there to the literature on transactional analysis was a short step, and of course it didn't hurt that I lived in Seattle in those years, where every conceivable form of the Rescue Game could be found in full swing. (The liveliest games of "Circular Firing Squad" in town just then were in the Marxist splinter parties, which I followed via their monthly newspapers. The sheer wallowing in ideological minutiae that went into identifying this or that party member as a deviationist would have impressed the stuffing out of medieval scholastic theologians.)

With impressive inevitability, in fact, every question about privilege in today's America gets turned into a game of "Pin the Tail on the Persecutor," in which one underprivileged group is blamed for the problems affecting another underprivileged group, and some group of overprivileged salary-class people show up to claim the Rescuer's role. That, in turn, leads to the third issue I want to consider here, which is the question of who benefits most from the habit of forcing all discussion of privilege in today's America into the straitjacket of the Rescue Game.

It's only fair to note that each of the three roles gets certain benefits, though these are distributed in a grossly unequal fashion. The only thing the people who are assigned the role of Persecutor get out of it is plenty of negative attention. Sometimes that's enough—it's a curious fact that hating and being hated can function as an intoxicant for some people—but this is rarely enough of an incentive to keep those assigned the Persecutor's role willing to play for long.

The benefits that go to people who are assigned the role of Victim are more substantial. Victims get to air their grievances in public, which is a rare event for the underprivileged, and they also get to engage in socially sanctioned bullying of people they don't like, which is an equally rare treat. That's all they get, though. In particular, despite reams of the usual rhetoric about redressing injustices and the like, the Victims are not supposed to do anything, or to expect the Rescuers to do anything, to change the conditions under which they live. The opportunities to air grievances and bully others are substitutes for substantive change, not—as they're usually billed—steps toward substantive change.

The vast majority of the benefits of the game, rather, go to the Rescuers. They're the ones who decide which team of Victims will get enough attention from Rescuers to start a game. They're the ones who enforce the rules, and thus see to it that Victims keep on being victimized and Persecutors keep on persecuting. Nor is it accidental that in every Rescue Game in American society today, the people who get the role of Rescuers are considerably higher on the ladder of social privilege than the people who get given the roles of Victims and Persecutors.

To some extent, in other words, the Rescue Game is a strategy that the overprivileged use to keep the underprivileged divided, so that the latter spend all their time and energy assailing one another rather than turning their attention on those who profit most from the situation. Such gimmicks are omnipresent in human societies, and a great deal of political magic focuses on setting up such arrangements, on the one hand, and disrupting them on the other. That political magic, to cite only one example, underlies the shrill insistence by salary-class pundits that everyone who voted for Trump must have been a racist. If wage-class white people and wage-class people of color got past that rhetoric and noticed that the interests they have in common far outweigh the interests they share with the salary-class interests that keep them at each other's throats, it would be game over for the salary-class ascendancy.

The Rescue Game can also be understood, however, as a magical ritual meant to sustain the self-image of the overprivileged as the Good People, the morally virtuous people. Ritual works by setting up a micro-cosm of the world and, within that microcosm, enacting whatever it is that you want yourself or others to experience in the world as a whole. In the ritual theater of the Rescue Game, the privileged enact a repetitive drama in which they get assigned the permanent role of sympathizers with the wronged and punishers of the bad. This allows them to defend themselves against the unwelcome recognition that their own behavior toward working people will not necessarily bear scrutiny in moral terms.

Yet there's usually more going on in such gimmicks than cold-blooded manipulation or magical action, and the present example is no exception. Look closely at the Rescue Game, in fact, and you can see straight down into one of the deep fissures that run through the heart of modern Western cultures.

Here again, an indirect approach is best, so we can start from the widespread conviction that certain common human emotions are evil and harmful and wrong, and the way to make a better world is to get rid of them. That belief is taken for granted throughout the industrial societies of the modern West, and it's been welded in place for a very long time, though—as we'll see in a moment—the particular emotions so labeled have varied from time to time. Just now, of course, the emotion at the center of this particular rogue's gallery is hate.

These days hate has roughly the same role in popular culture that original sin has in traditional Christian theology. If you want to slap the worst imaginable label on an organization, you call it a hate group. If you want to push a category of discourse straight into the realm of the utterly unacceptable, you call it hate speech. If you're speaking in public and you want to be sure that everyone in the crowd will beam approval at you, all you have to do is denounce hate.

That was what underlay the vapid slogan used by Hillary Clinton's presidential campaign in 2016: LOVE TRUMPS HATE. I hope that none of my readers are under the illusion that Clinton and her inner circle were primarily motivated by love—well, other than Clinton's love of power and the Democrats' love of the privileges and payouts they could expect from four more years of control of the White House; and of course Trump and the Republicans were just as crazy in love with the same things. The fact that Clinton's marketing flacks thought that the slogan just quoted would have an impact on the election shows just how pervasive the assumption I'm discussing has become in our culture.

Now of course most people these days, confronted with the sort of thing I've just written, are likely to respond, "Wait, are you saying that hate is good?"—as though the only alternatives available are condemning something as absolutely bad or praising it as absolutely good. Let's set that simplistic reaction to one side for the moment, and ask a different question: what happens when people decide that some common human emotion is evil and harmful and wrong, and decide that the way to make a better world is to get rid of it?

As it turns out, we have a very good idea what happens in this case, because a first-rate example of the phenomenon completed its historical trajectory on the edge of living memory. The example I have in mind is the attitude, pervasive in the English-speaking world from the middle of the nineteenth century to the middle of the twentieth, that sex was the root of all evil.

The Victorian horror of sexual desire has been mocked so mercilessly in recent decades that many people these days have forgotten just how seriously it was taken at the time. During its heyday, people in Britain and America loudly proclaimed exactly the same attitudes toward sex that their great-grandchildren now display toward hate. If you wanted to define anything as utterly beyond the pale, you just had to label it as "immoral"—in the jargon of the time, this meant "sexual"—and the vast majority of people were expected to recoil from it in horror. No political campaign back in the day, as far as I know, used the slogan PURITY TRUMPS IMMORALITY, but then political sloganeering hadn't yet decayed into the kind of empty mouthing of buzzwords on display at present. The sentiment was certainly there.

By the way, yes, I know that comparing current attitudes toward hate with Victorian attitudes toward sex will inspire instant pushback from a good many readers. After all, sex is natural and normal and healthy, while hate is evil and harmful and wrong, right? Here again, it's easy to lose track of the fact that people a century and a quarter ago—most likely including your ancestors, dear reader, if they happened to live in the English-speaking world—saw things the other way around. To them, hate was an ordinary emotion that most people had under certain circumstances, but sexual desire was beyond the pale: beastly, horrid, filthy, and so on through an impressive litany of unpleasant adjectives.

It was also something that all of them experienced. That's where the comparison begins to bite, because insisting that sexual desire was beastly, horrid, filthy, and so forth didn't make it go away, or deprive it of its substantial role in motivating human behavior. It just meant that people got hypocritical about it. Some pretended that it wasn't there.

Some insisted that in certain sharply defined contexts—for example, within the bounds of legal marriage—it wasn't the same, no, of course not, how could you suggest such a horrid thing? Some pursued any of the other dodges, and there were plenty of them, that allowed people to pretend that they weren't getting sexually aroused and acting on their arousal when, in fact, that's what they were doing.

That's what happens whenever people decide a normal human emotion is unacceptable and insist that good people don't experience it. A culture of pretense, hypocrisy, and evasion—a Pallid Mask to rival the one that appears in Robert W. Chambers' tales of *The King in Yellow*—springs up to allow them to vent the unacceptable emotion on some set of acceptable targets without admitting that they are doing so. That's what emerged in Victorian society once people convinced themselves that sexual desire was the root of all evil, and it's what has emerged in our time as people have convinced themselves that hate fills the same role. In a very real sense, these days, hate is the new sex.

If you have any doubts concerning this, dear reader, watch the way that the same people who were sporting LOVE TRUMPS HATE bumper stickers in 2016 have talked about Donald Trump and his supporters ever since. Take the rhetoric currently being flung by well-off Democratic voters at Trump supporters, swap out the ethnic labels for any other set you choose, and you'll have a hard time telling it apart from the rantings of any other group of bigots.

The class dimension of all this rhetoric about hate, by the way, is one of the most telling things about it. Back in the Victorian era, the privileged classes defined themselves as the Good People, the moral, virtuous, pure people, which in the language of the time meant the people who supposedly didn't have sexual desires. They accordingly defined their social inferiors as beastly, horrid, filthy—that is to say, sexual beings. Nowadays, what defines the Good People has changed, but the class bigotry hasn't. The privileged people claim to be the ones who don't hate, and define their inferiors as hate-filled bigots. The relative behavior of the two groups, it bears repeating, does not exactly justify this claim.

For that matter, watch the way that the American media and the privileged classes of this country have been utterly fixated on the person of Donald Trump since 2016. In my memory—and I've watched new presidents take office since the days of Richard Nixon—I've never seen so obsessive a concern with someone who, after all, is simply an elected official. It reminds me, to be precise, of the way that Victorian prudes would travel miles by train to be shocked and offended by some display or other of sexuality. I'd like to suggest that in this case, as in that one, the shock and the offense are filmy garments that very imperfectly cover a seething, sweaty mass of unacknowledged desire.

Across the river from the city where I now live, in the upscale hipster neighborhood along Providence's old waterfront, light poles right after the inauguration sprouted stickers showing the president's face and the slogan, TRUMP HATES YOU. Literally speaking, the claim was absurd—there's no reason to think that Donald Trump was aware of the existence of the people who put up and viewed those stickers, and we don't even have to talk about the likelihood that he felt any particular emotion toward them—but in another sense, it's profoundly revealing.

When people don't want to deal with an emotion they're feeling, one very common dodge they use is to insist that they're not feeling it— no, no, it's that awful person over there who's feeling it, toward them. In the Victorian era, that dodge racked up plenty of overtime, as people who couldn't cope with the fact that they had sexual feelings projected those feelings onto others, and then labeled the others beastly, horrid, filthy, and so forth, for supposedly having those feelings. The same thing is going on here. The people who make and post those stickers can't just come out and say I HATE TRUMP—that admission would consign them once and for all, in their own eyes, to the category of Bad People—so they project their own hatred onto the person they hate, and convince themselves that *he* hates *them*.

Notice, furthermore, how this feeds into the utter fascination with which so many people on the leftward end of the political spectrum hang on Donald Trump's every word and action. Seen through the fun-house mirror of their projected emotions, he's the equivalent of a naked couple in Victorian England having hot sex right there in the middle of the street. He's acting out their dearest fantasy, hating other people right out there in public—how can they possibly look away? In effect, they put an apostrophe into Clinton's slogan, and made it read LOVE TRUMP'S HATE. Covertly, in the silent hours of the night, they do.

That's the problem with taking an ordinary human emotion, slapping a pallid mask over it, and insisting that it has to be gotten rid of in order to make the world perfect. Make something forbidden and you make it desirable. Take a normal human emotional state—one that everyone experiences—and make it forbidden, and you guarantee that the desire to violate the taboo will take on overwhelming power. That's why, after spending their days subject to the pervasive tone policing of contemporary life, in which every utterance gets scrutinized for the least trace of anything that could be called hateful, so many people in today's world don internet aliases and go to online forums where they can blurt out anything, no matter how nasty. They're doing it in the same spirit with which Victorian men went to brothels and Victorian women arranged covert assignations with muscular young stablehands.

Nor, if history is any guide, will the return of the repressed be limited to such hole-and-corner expressions for long. Victorian sexual repressiveness, after all, eventually gave rise to the Sexual Revolution, which swung to the opposite extreme with an equal lack of balance. In the same way, today's attempt to repress hate could quite easily give rise to a Revolution of Hate, in which people wallow in hatred the way libertines in the 1960s and 1970s wallowed in sex. The identical rhetoric of liberation, of being natural, of casting off the straitjacket of an outdated morality, would serve equally well for both.

It may come as a surprise to those who've read this far that I don't favor this latter possibility. The opposite of one bad idea, after all, is usually another bad idea, just as the fact that dying of thirst is bad for you doesn't make drowning good for you. Whether we're talking about sex or anything else, there's a space somewhere between "not enough" and "too much," between pathological repression and pathological expression, that's considerably healthier than either of the extremes. I'm going to risk causing my more sensitive readers to clutch their smelling salts and faint on the nearest sofa by suggesting that the same thing's true of hate.

We all feel it, you know, and you know what? Sometimes that's appropriate. There are actions done by human beings to other human beings that deserve a more robust response than the sort of simpering evasions that are acceptable today—"Oh, isn't that sad," "I'm sure he didn't mean to do it," "It's not fair to pass judgment," and so on, all the vacuous nonsense by which we're expected to pretend that actions don't have consequences and people don't bear responsibility for their decisions. Au contraire, there are actions that deserve to be condemned, judgments that need to be made, and individuals for whom the hot flame of fury or the frozen wall of hate are, from time to time, appropriate responses.

Does that mean that every hatred and every expression of hatred is appropriate? Of course not. Hate is like sex; there are times, places, and contexts where it's appropriate, but there are many, many others where it's not. You can recognize its place in life without having to act it out on every occasion—and in fact, the more conscious you are of its place in life, the more completely you acknowledge it and give it its due, the less likely you are to get blindsided by it. As magical philosophy has taught for a long time, that's true of sex, and it's true of hate. What you refuse to acknowledge controls you. What you acknowledge, you can learn to control.

Now of course doing this involves challenging deep-seated cultural imperatives. It's one of the basic presuppositions of our culture that we're supposed to become perfect, and the way to become perfect, we're told, is to amputate whatever part of ourselves keeps us from being perfect. The last sixteen hundred years or so of moral philosophy in the Western world have been devoted to this theme: find the thing that's causing us to be evil, find some way to chop it off, and then we'll all behave like plaster saints. The mere fact that it never works hasn't yet slowed down the endless profusion of attempts to try it again.

Yet there's another dimension to this pattern of failure, and it inevitably circles back to the class conflicts we've discussed already. When perfection has been defined as the removal of some part of being human, and the privileged classes have defined themselves as the Good People in the usual manner, some ritual formula has to be found to permit the Good People to do whatever it is that Good People aren't supposed to do, without compromising either their status or their ability to preen themselves on their superior virtue. Anthropologists of an earlier generation used to say that every taboo has its exception, and the rule certainly applies here. The Good People today are as much in need of an excuse to hate as the Good People of Queen Victoria's time were in need of an excuse to have sex, and the Rescue Game is one of the principal ways that the salary class gives itself permission to hate.

This is an important part of what underlies the insistence on the part of the corporate media, and the salary class more generally, that Trump and all his followers are motivated solely by racism, or some other currently unfashionable form of prejudice. It's probably necessary to unpack the dubious logic of this claim again, so that we can get past that and see what's actually being said. Does Trump have racial prejudices? No doubt; most Americans do. Do his followers share his prejudices? Again, no doubt some of them do—not all his followers are white, after all, a point that the leftward end of the media has been desperately trying to obscure. Let's assume for the sake of argument, though, that Trump and his followers do indeed share an assortment of racial prejudices. Does that fact, if it is a fact, prove that racism must by definition be the only thing that makes Trump appeal to his followers?

Of course it proves nothing of the kind. You could use the same illogic to insist that since Trump enjoys steak, and many of his followers share that taste, the people who follow him must be entirely motivated by hatred for vegetarians. Something that white Americans generally don't discuss, though I'm told that people of color are acutely aware of it, is that racial issues simply aren't that important to white people in this country nowadays. The frantic defense of racial bigotry that typified the Jim Crow era is rare these days outside of the white-supremacist fringe. What has replaced it, by and large, are habits that most white people consider to be no big deal—and you don't get a mass movement going in the teeth of the political establishment by appealing to attitudes that the people who hold them consider to be no big deal.

Behind the shouts of "Racist!" directed at the Trump campaign by a great many affluent white liberals, rather, lies a rather different reality. Accusations of racism can play many roles in contemporary American discourse, and we've already discussed the way that it serves to divide the wage class against itself for the benefit of the salary class. Quite often, though, when affluent white liberals make that accusation, on the other hand, it's a dog whistle.

I should probably explain that last phrase for the benefit of those of my readers who don't speak fluent internet. A dog whistle, in online jargon, is a turn of phrase or a trope that expresses some form of bigotry while giving the bigot plausible deniability. Back in the twentieth century, for example, the phrase "states' rights" was a dog whistle; the rights under discussion amounted to the right of white Southerners to impose racial discrimination on their black neighbors, but the White Citizens Council spokesmen who waxed rhapsodic about states' rights never said that in so many words. That there are serious issues about the balance of power between states and the federal government that have nothing do with race, and thus got roundly ignored by both sides of the struggle, is just one more irony in a situation that had no shortage of them already.

In the same way, the word *racist* in the mouths of the pundits and politicians who apply it so liberally to the Trump campaign is a dog whistle for something they don't want to talk about in so many words. What they mean by it, of course, is "wage-class American."

Consider the 2016 standoff in southeastern Oregon between militia members and federal officials. While that was ongoing, wags in the blogosphere and the hip end of the media started referring to the militia members as "Y'all-Qaeda." Attentive readers may happen to know that none of the militia members came from the South, the only part of the United States where "y'all" is the second person plural pronoun. To the best of my knowledge, all of them came from the dryland West, where "y'all" is no more common than it is on the streets of Manhattan or San Francisco. Why, then, did the label catch on so quickly and get the predictable sneering laughter of the salary class?

It caught on the way it did and got that laugh because most members of the salary class in the United States love to apply a specific stereotype to the entire American wage class. You know that stereotype as well as I do, dear reader. It's a fat, pink-faced, gap-toothed Southern good ol' boy in jeans and a greasy T-shirt, watching a NASCAR race on television from a broken-down sofa, with one hand stuffed elbow deep into a bag of Cheez Doodles and the other fondling a shotgun, while a Confederate flag hangs on the wall behind him and a Klan outfit waits in the bedroom closet. As a description of wage-earning Americans in general, that stereotype is as crass, as bigoted, and as politically motivated as any of the racial and sexual stereotypes that so many people these days are ready to denounce—but if you mention this, affluent white liberals who would sooner impale themselves on their own designer corkscrews than mention African Americans and watermelons in the same breath will insist at the top of their lungs that it's not a stereotype, it's the way "those people" really are.

Here as so often, blaming the victims is much easier than talking about who's actually responsible for the current state of affairs, who benefits from it, and what the real issues are. When that conversation is one that people who have a privileged role in shaping public discourse desperately don't want to have, blaming the victim is also an effective diversionary tactic, and accordingly it gets plenty of use in the media these days.

To speak in terms introduced earlier in this book, that diversionary tactic is the goal of the magic being worked by the privileged classes in today's America, the beneficiaries of the "magician state" that Couliano anatomized. Magic is a funny thing, though, and tolerably often it obeys a curious variant of Newton's famous law: every magical action generates an unequal and opposite reaction. To follow that reaction along the winding paths that helped put Donald Trump in the White House in 2016 is to plunge into the strangest and most important dimension of the magical politics of our time, because the magic that shaped the 2016 election and its aftermath wasn't limited to the bowdlerized, rationalized, pasteurized magic of advertising copywriters and public relations flacks.

During and after the 2016 election campaign, to be precise, a substantial number of people on both sides of the political divide were practicing magic in the full, robust, unabashed sense of the word. They were studying occult teachings and performing magical rituals in an attempt to influence the political situation in the United States. It is to them that we now turn.

4

The Orange Sign

The Coming of the Kek Wars

The gate below opened and shut, and I crept shaking to my door and bolted it, but I knew no bolts, no locks, could keep that creature out who was coming for the Yellow Sign. And now I heard him moving very softly along the hall. And now he was at the door, and the bolts rotted at his touch.

FROM "THE YELLOW SIGN," *THE KING IN YELLOW*

Since the 2016 election, a great deal of talk has circulated claiming that sinister occult influences were behind the rise of Donald Trump. Much of that talk focused on Steve Bannon, who played an important role in Trump's election campaign and was briefly in his administration, and the Traditionalist movement, which has been Bannon's spiritual home for many years. Much of it also fixated on Russia, the great bogeyman of the American salary class ever since Vladimir Putin took power and snatched various tempting goodies out of the jaws of an assortment of Fortune 500 corporations. Several books from big corporate publishers have tried to explain the outcome of the 2016 election in terms that would not seem out of place in an occult adventure story from a pulp magazine a century ago, complete with sinister Russian masterminds managing it all—though there's been a notable shortage of the square-jawed action heroes that used to feature in such tales.

Russians, Traditionalists, and most of the other bogeypersons of today's Left had very little to do with what happened in 2016, and even less to do with the way that events have unfolded since that year's election. Even so, there's a point to taking a look at Traditionalism and its tangled interactions with the political sphere, past and present. That glance will make it easier to make sense of the very different landscape of magical politics that shaped the rise of Donald Trump.

To understand Traditionalism it's important to begin with the much larger and more successful movement it was born to oppose. The Theosophical Society, founded in New York City in 1875, was the first modern organization to teach occultism in public, and it found an enthusiastic welcome from people all over the world who were dissatisfied with the dogmatic Christianity and equally dogmatic scientific atheism that made up the sole options Western industrial civilization offered its inmates just then. Unlike the more secretive occult organizations that preceded it, most of which were strictly apolitical, Theosophy was also well over to the leftward side of the nineteenth-century political spectrum: it supported the women's suffrage movement and a variety of other left-wing causes.

During the heyday of Theosophy, accordingly, a good many conservative occultists set out to create something on the other side of the political spectrum. Three of those became significant factors in twentieth-century alternative culture. In central Europe, the one that mattered was Ariosophy—a reworking of Theosophical ideas to fit fashionable notions of white racial superiority. You've heard of Ariosophy, though not necessarily under that name; the Nazi Party started out as a political action group sponsored by an Ariosophical lodge, the Thule Society, and most Nazi ideology was straight-up Ariosophy. Nicholas Goodrick-Clarke's *The Occult Roots of Nazism* is the go-to volume if you want to know more about that.

In North America, a very different movement coalesced around an offshoot of Theosophy called the Ascended Masters teachings, one of the least studied and most significant currents in contemporary American popular religion. Those teachings, and most of the people who follow them, embrace classic American conservatism of the "God, guns, and guts made America great!" variety rather than anything more extreme. There have been a few attempts over the years to organize a political movement or party around the Ascended Masters teachings, but those have uniformly fizzled; most followers of the Ascended Masters, if they're politically active at all, simply vote for conservative candidates and leave it at that.

Traditionalism was the third such movement, and it differed from the others at least as much as they differed from each other. It emerged in France and Italy after the First World War, with the French occultist René Guenon as its leading figure, and it had intellectual credentials the other two movements lacked. Rather than claiming to have inherited secret teachings from Germanic prehistory or received them from the Ascended Masters, the Traditionalists argued that they were hiding in plain sight, in the great religious and mystical traditions of the world. Guenon and other Traditionalist authors thus wrote commentaries on those traditions and blended their insights with a political vision rooted in classic European conservatism.

Then there was Julius Evola. Few people these days, even among those with conservative views, can read a book by Evola without at least once feeling a powerful urge to fling it across the room. If Evola is watching his posthumous career from some cold Hyperborean summit, he must be laughing mordantly, because this is exactly the reception he wanted. He loathed the modern world and everything it stood for, and his icy contempt for modernity led him to construct an ethos and a spirituality that flies in the face of everything the modern Western world considers good, valid, and true. It didn't help that he condemned Mussolini's government for not being fascist enough, spent the last part of the Second World War as an officer in the Waffen-SS, and became a major source of inspiration for neofascist political, cultural, and spiritual movements once the war was over.

Evola gets most of the attention from critics of Traditionalism on the leftward end of today's culture precisely because he's such an easy target. Most Traditionalists have read at least some of his writings, which makes them easy targets, too. The point that gets swept under the rug in the resulting denunciation is that the political ideas of Evola's fascist period find few takers among Traditionalists these days. His most influential book on politics, *Ride the Tiger,* argues for strict political noninvolvement as the only viable option for the "aristocrats of the soul" in a decadent age. (Clearly that wasn't Steve Bannon's view.)

None of the three movements just outlined succeeded in overthrowing Theosophy. The Theosophical Society did that job all by itself by building up a messianic cult around Jiddu Krishnamurti, and went through a near-total collapse in 1929 after Krishnamurti renounced the role crafted for him and walked away. Ariosophy imploded far more messily when it hitched its destiny to Adolf Hitler and rose and fell along with Nazi Germany. The other two movements didn't make the same mistake and have thrived in a quiet way ever since, the Ascended Masters teachings among ordinary Americans in flyover country, Traditionalism among disaffected conservative intellectuals all over the world.

If you happened to be a disaffected conservative intellectual with a taste for politics, the reaction against the domination of the salary class was the place to be in the early twenty-first century. That was how Steve Bannon found his way into the Trump campaign in 2016. Bannon is a Traditionalist, but an eccentric one, for he considers ordinary, deplorable wage-class Americans to be among the guardians of Tradition—a viewpoint you will not find in Guenon, Evola, or any other significant Traditionalist author. That view was what framed the strategy he crafted for Trump's first presidential campaign: he advised Trump to ignore the mouthpieces of the salary class and go directly to the masses. Trump did so, and won.

Of course Bannon is not the only figure with Traditionalist

connections to get involved in politics in recent years. Aleksandr Dugin, a leading Russian Traditionalist, is widely touted as one of Vladimir Putin's advisers, and Brazilian Traditionalist Olavo de Carvalho has the same role in the inner circle of maverick Brazilian President Jair Bolsonaro. Benjamin Teitelbaum's useful if sometimes strident 2020 volume *War for Eternity* does a respectable job of chronicling the connections, and also the conflicts, among these figures.

Yet there's nothing especially unusual about the Traditionalist presence in contemporary politics. Whenever existing political arrangements come apart and outsiders find their way into positions of influence and power, a noticeable fraction of those outsiders have connections to alternative spirituality. That was how the Theosophist Henry A. Wallace became an important figure in Franklin Roosevelt's administration in the 1930s, for example, as one of FDR's vice presidents and later Secretary of Agriculture, and it's also how Julius Evola himself had a brief role as an adviser to Mussolini's regime. Both men were outsiders with new ideas at a time when breaking the stranglehold of the failed economic dogmas of the 1920s on public life was the one thing that mattered. That I know of, there's no evidence that Wallace performed magical rituals for the benefit of the New Deal or that Evola did so for Mussolini, and I have yet to see any evidence that Bannon did anything of the kind for Donald Trump.

Yet there were people performing magical rituals for Trump's benefit during and after the 2016 presidential campaign, and their story is an essential part of the Trump phenomenon. To understand how that happened and why, it's going to be necessary to take a deeper plunge into the territory that Ioan Couliano explored—the territory where politics and magic become two sides of the same strange coin.

We can begin that exploration by recognizing that magic always has a political context. Magic is the politics of the excluded. It's also, in an inversion of a kind typical in such situations, the politics of the excluders. Eras when magic flourishes, in other words, are eras when the division between those who make the decisions and those who suffer the consequences runs deeper than usual: that is to say, times like the present.

Let's start with the magic of the excluded. When most people have at least a little influence on day to day politics, and have some chance of getting their needs heard and their grievances addressed, they tend to neglect magic. This is true even if their influence is limited and others have a great deal more than they do. For example, the golden age of African American folk magic was between 1900 and 1945—the period when Jim Crow laws were most savagely enforced across the American South, and various devices were used to deny African Americans the civil rights they had theoretically been granted after the Civil War—and built on magical traditions developed by African Americans during the era of slavery. In those eras when African Americans had some access to political power—between 1865 and 1900, in the wake of Reconstruction, and from 1945 on, in the wake of the Civil Rights Movement—their interest in magic waned.

This makes perfect sense if you understand magic the way that operative mages do. Magic, as we've seen, is the art and science of causing changes in consciousness in accordance with will. If you are denied access to any other source of power, you can still exercise power over your own consciousness. What's more, if you do that and get good at it, you'll find that some of the techniques you use to shape your own thoughts and feelings will also shape the thoughts and feelings of others, with or without their consent or knowledge. Magic thus becomes the logical fallback option for those who are denied any other way of pursuing their goals or seeking redress for their grievances. Periods in which magic becomes popular, then, are periods when more people than usual are excluded from whatever mechanisms their societies provide for seeking redress of grievances.

That process of exclusion is itself a magical act, a set of arrangements to cause changes in consciousness in accordance with the will of those who benefited from the existing order of things, and in the next chapter we'll discuss how that works and how it fails. To every magical action, however, there is an unequal and not-quite-opposite reaction, and so the magic that made certain policies look inevitable and beneficent to the salary class generated an inescapable blowback elsewhere. Part of that blowback came from the working classes that took the brunt of the policies just named, and part of it came from other sectors of society that were shut out of the benefits of the bipartisan policy consensus and forced to carry a disproportionate share of the costs. Another element of it, though, unfolded from a policy that elites always embrace sooner or later: the habit of making sure that the educational system produces more people trained for managerial tasks than the society's institutions can absorb.

Why should elites do this? For them, at least in the short term, the advantages are obvious. If you're going to entrust the running of society to a hierarchy of flunkeys who are allowed to rise up from the underprivileged masses but are never quite allowed to join the overprivileged elite—and this, of course, is the normal condition of a complex society—you need to enforce rigid loyalty to the system and the ideas it considers acceptable. The most reliable way to this is to set candidates for flunkeyhood against each other in a savage competition that most will lose.

As your prospective flunkeys climb over one another, kicking and clawing their way toward a sharply limited number of positions of relative wealth and influence, any weakness they display becomes a weapon in the hands of rivals. You thus can count on getting the best, the brightest, and—above all—the most obedient, those who have erased from their minds any tendency to think any thought not preapproved by the conventional wisdom. Your candidates will be earnest, idealistic, committed, ambitious, if that's what you want them to be. Ask them to be something else and you'll get that, too, because under the smiling and well-groomed facade you've got a bunch of panicked conformists whose one stark terror is that they will somehow fail to please their masters.

If you want to see that process in action, watch the way that people of color who want to become members of the upper ranks of the salary class are expected to systematically discard everything that sets them apart from other members of the salary class. (Note that I'm not talking about athletes, musicians, writers, university professors, or others in the entertainment sector, who are expected to flaunt their differences from the salary-class norm, so they can be patronized accordingly.) If it's not a matter of raw biology—for example, skin color—out it goes: attitudes, values, lifestyles, all must conform to the accepted salary-class template. There is no room for anything but the most harmlessly cosmetic of variations.

This isn't simply a matter of ordinary conformism, though of course that's involved as well. It's also a matter of magical ritual. To members of the salary class in today's industrial societies, their attitudes and lifestyles are the hallmarks of the glorious progressive future that everyone will eventually embrace, whether they want to or not. Every person who embraces these things in a ritually correct manner in advance of that final triumph, discarding their own values and preferences in the process, hastens the coming of the allegedly utopian future where people of every continent and gender and ethnic group will all embrace exactly the same rigidly prescribed set of beliefs, and take up exactly the same suffocatingly narrow range of lifestyles. Those who aspire to salary-class status, above all, must prove their fitness for that status by ritually enacting the supposedly perfect future in the ceremonial spaces of their university classrooms and office cubicles.

It's the losers in that competition who matter here, though. There are always some of them, and in modern America there are a lot of them: young men and women who got shoved aside in the stampede for those positions of wealth and influence, and didn't even get the various consolation prizes our society offers the more successful end of the also-rans. They're the ones who for one reason or another—lack of money, lack of talent, lack of desire—didn't take all the right classes, do all the right extracurricular activities, pass all the right tests, think all the right thoughts, and so fell by the wayside. It's a familiar subculture for me, not least because I belong to it; a great many occultists these days do.

Not all of the losers in question live in their moms' basements and spend their days playing video games, but a significant number do. In today's America, remember, jobs are scarce, rents have been artificially inflated to an absurd degree, and what used to be the normal trajectory toward an independent adult life has been slammed shut for a very large number of young people. So for several decades now, those who have been shut out, the educated failures, gathered online, played video games, and frequented online forums such as "the chans"—websites such as 4chan and 8chan—where posts are anonymous, the rules that govern acceptable discourse among the respectable classes no longer apply, and the more offensive to the privileged an idea is, the better it goes over.

That's usually what happens when an elite makes the mistake of educating far more people than it's willing to employ. Go look at the long history of revolutions and you'll find that far more often than not, the people who overthrow governments and bring nations crashing down are the precise equivalent of today's basement brigade: people with educations but no opportunities, losers in the struggle for prestige and wealth, who figure out how to weaponize their outsider status in one way or another. One of the things that makes the losers so dangerous in such a setting is that they have a freedom their successful classmates lack: the freedom to think and say whatever they want. In the struggle for success, remember, any least sign of straying from the acceptable is a weapon in the hands of your rivals, and will be used ruthlessly to shove you aside and take your place. (Watch students at prestigious U.S. universities looking for any pretext to accuse each other of racism or sexism if you want to watch a fine example of this process in action.)

Those who drop out of the struggle don't have to submit to the suffocating conformism demanded of their more successful peers, and inevitably make use of that freedom in ways that offend the conventionally minded. That's harmless if the conventional wisdom works. It stops being harmless in a hurry when the policies embraced by the aristocracy have disastrous consequences for too many people outside the self-referential bubble of elite culture. Smart aristocrats recognize this, and pay attention to the way their policies affect the lives of the majority, but here in America we don't have smart aristocrats. We have clueless aristocrats who've barricaded themselves inside a hermetically sealed echo chamber from which any talk of the downsides of the approved policies has been carefully excluded.

What happens in situations like this is that the losers become the only ones willing to talk about the things that matter most to a great many people. That means, in turn, that whatever ideology the losers happen to embrace may just become the guiding vision of radical political change, and if the change goes far enough, that ideology can end up imposed on a nation. If you're lucky, the losers in question might embrace democratic nationalism, and you get a successful democracy such as Ireland or India. If you're not lucky, the losers in question might embrace a more toxic ideology, and you get Nazi Germany or the Soviet Union.

And the losers we're discussing? That's where the alt-right comes into the story.

If you happen to be interested in the history of ideas, as I am, one of the most fascinating events in the last dozen years or so has been the twilight of Reagan-era pseudoconservatism and the first tentative gropings toward the revival of an authentic conservatism: that is to say, a political and social movement that actually conserves something. The pseudoconservatives of the Reagan and post-Reagan era adopted nearly every major policy of Franklin Roosevelt's New Deal—deficit spending on the grand scale, government subsidies for private industry, endlessly expanding entitlement programs for the middle class, endlessly expanding federal regulations, a foreign policy obsessed with military intervention overseas, and the rest of it—while tossing the occasional crumb to religious conservatives and a few other pressure groups on the right.

It's hardly an exaggeration to say that anyone who proposed today's "conservative" policies in a GOP county convention in 1950, say, would have been thrown out of the meeting with enough force to leave buttock-shaped dents in the sidewalk. Until recently, though, the only alternatives to that faux-conservative ideology were, on the one hand, the Neoconservatives, who simply doubled down on all of American pseudoconservatism's worst features, and on the other, a gaggle of extremist religious zealots and free-market libertarians whose idea of conservatism was to pursue their own arbitrary utopian fantasies with a doctrinaire enthusiasm that more than matched that of the Marxists they so cordially hated.

That started to change in 2007, when Curtis Yarvin, blogging under the name Mencius Moldbug, began attracting attention online with a set of ideas that have come to be called "Neoreaction"—essentially, classic nineteenth-century European reactionary politics retooled for early twenty-first-century conditions, complete with an enthusiasm for absolute monarchy and a rejection of the whole range of democratic values. Neoreaction had a modest vogue in those online circles where the excluded spend their ample spare time, and thereafter it quickly lost its novelty and settled back into the same underworld of longshot social causes where distributism, social threefolding, democratic syndicalism, and the like have their home. It succeeded, though, in punching a hole through the pseudoconservative orthodoxies of our time and raising hard questions about what a genuine alternative to the status quo would look like.

It also introduced a useful term into what would become the vocabulary of the alt-right: "the Cathedral." This was Yarvin's term for the enforced consensus of the mainstream, the set of values and beliefs that justify the existing order of society and, not coincidentally, the privileged place of the managerial aristocracy in that order. It's a brilliant coinage, because it catches the devout faith and the moral fervor with which believers in the conventional wisdom of our time rally around the things they believe. At the same time, of course, a cathedral isn't simply a set of ideas. It's also an institution that deploys plenty of influence and wealth, and it is the visible expression of a hierarchy in which believers and heretics alike have their strictly defined places.

Mind you, there are plenty of things not to like about Neoreaction, and some of the things that followed in its wake were even more toxic. Of course various reworkings of fascism and national socialism got a word in—the cultural mainstream has put so much effort into portraying Hitler as the ultimate antithesis of today's elite values that it was inevitable that some would stray down that self-defeating path. The Traditionalists got their share of air time, with Julius Evola in particular becoming a fave of the newborn alt-right, and so did more recently minted ideologies. The one thing they all had in common was that they were utterly unacceptable to America's salary-class aristocracy—and of course that's the one feature they needed to have. Those who have been discarded and despised by the gatekeepers of the status quo will only be interested in ideologies that those same gatekeepers have placed beyond the pale.

The alt-right scene remains just as diverse today as it was before Trump began his first campaign, and there isn't yet a consensus ideology among the losers we've been discussing. The label "alt-right" is a label for a grab bag of contending notions, not a specific set of proposals. Here again, the corporate media's loud insistence that the alt-right is all about racism is straightforward disinformation, meant to cover up the far more threatening challenge the alt-right poses to the pallid mask that covers the ascendancy of the salary class. What that challenge was—we'll get to that in due time.

Thus one crucial wild card in play, once a society has pupped a sufficiently large batch of losers, is which ideology will become central to the opposition to the elite, and in the present case that hasn't been decided yet. Since so much of the alt-right closed ranks around the Trump campaign when that got under way in 2015, it's entirely possible that something not too far from old-fashioned democratic nationalism may be the ideology that comes out on top in the current situation, in which case the long-term results could be fairly good—although it's still quite possible that something more toxic might result instead.

The other crucial wild card is the choice of a basic strategy. If revolutionary warfare happens to catch the fancy of the excluded, and they can make common cause with a demographic sector that includes a lot of the rank and file of the military and a lot of military vets, then there's a good chance that your society will plunge into civil war, and a lot of people will die. If it's terrorism that catches their fancy, a smaller number of people will die much more uselessly—terrorism is great for working off your martyr complex but it almost always fails. (How many terrorist organizations can you name that actually succeeded in their political aims? It's a very, very short list.)

But there are other options as well, and one of them is magic.

Magic is extremely well suited to politics, since human beings in the mass are easily swayed by symbols and ritual actions. Look at the way that content-free incantations such as "Hope," "Change," and "Yes We Can" helped catapult Barack Obama into the presidency, and you can grasp some hint of the power of magic in politics. What makes magic an extraordinarily potent force, though, is that it doesn't require the kind of immense marketing budget that Obama's campaign used to sell their bland and smiling product to the voters. It can be done on a shoe-string budget by a few part-time people if it's done cleverly enough, and with enough mastery of the principles of magic.

It was in 2015, or so I've read, that several frequent habitués of "the chans" encountered a particular school of modern magic, brought it back to their favorite online forums, and started talking enthusiastically about it. The particular form of magic they introduced to the basement brigade is called chaos magic, and thereby hangs a tale.

It so happens that every few decades someone tries to bridge the gap between science and magic by coming up with a version of magic that borrows concepts from current trends in science, and deep-sixes those elements of traditional Western occultism that scientists won't tolerate. It never succeeds in bridging the gap, because modern science from the seventeenth century onward has defined its identity in opposition to occultism, and any time the mages come up with something that comes too close to science, the scientists simply move the goal posts. Yet the systems of magic created by these efforts tolerably often work well in practice, and can develop an extensive following.

In the nineteenth century, for example, physicists theorized that light consisted of wave patterns in the ether, a hypothetical substance filling the universe. Occultists jumped on the label "ether" and borrowed it as a label for the subtle omnipresent life force of magical theory—that's spelled *qi* in Chinese, *ki* in Japanese, *prana* in Sanskrit, and so on through the roster of the world's languages. (As far as I know, the only languages on Earth that don't have a word for this commonly recognized reality are the dominant languages of the industrial nations of the West. Is that accidental? If you believe that, I have an etheric bridge to sell you.)

In response to the borrowing of their term by occultists, scientists dropped the ether like a hot rock. Instead, light became probability waves moving through four-dimensional spacetime. What differentiates "four-dimensional spacetime" from "the ether"? Purely that the former enables scientists to place the familiar distance between their disciplines and the occult. I suspect from time to time that if occultists started making a big deal of the fact that the Earth revolves around the Sun, scientists would rediscover the joys of a geocentric cosmos.

Chaos magic thus emerged in the usual way in the late 1970s, just as the current generation of radical scientific materialists were beginning to hit their stride, and it's telling that the *bêtes noires* of those same radical scientific materialists—notably, the real existence of gods and spirits, on the one hand, and the efficacy of astrology on the other—were also heatedly rejected by the early chaos mages. The goal of the founders of the new magic was, as usual, the development of magical systems free of old-fashioned superstition, and thus notionally acceptable to people who have bought into the worldview of contemporary science.

The result was an approach to magic that treats gods, spirits, and other magical beings as wholly imaginary constructs used by human beings to focus their innate magical energies. Does it work? Sure, within the limits it sets for itself. As an unabashed practitioner of traditional Western occultism, I find that chaos magic reminds me forcefully of lite beer, in contrast to the rich dark brew of the sort of magic I prefer— but of course there are people who like lite beer. In magic, as so many other things, personal tastes are what they are, and there's no such thing as One True Way. I know people who use chaos magic and get good results with it.

Two core elements of chaos magic, however, made it particularly well suited to the culture of the chans, and a third turned out to have decisive importance in the way things worked out once what we may as well call the Kek Wars broke out. The first of these elements is that the methods of chaos magic mesh well with certain aspects of today's online outsider culture. The basic working tool of common or garden variety chaos magic is the sigil, a symbolic image or pattern used to represent the intention of a magical working. Internet memes by and large make good sigils, and some of them make very good hypersigils—this is the chaos magic term for a sigil used by a group of people with a shared intention.

Second, while chaos magic takes just as much hard work to master as any other kind of magic, the simplified nature of its theory and practice makes it fairly easy for beginners to pick up some degree of basic competence at it very quickly. In particular, a fairly modest amount of reading and practice will enable the enthusiastic beginner to learn how to create suitable sigils and charge them with magical energy using any of several simple methods. That made it possible for the chans to become a chaos magic boot camp for thousands of young people who'd been discarded by the system and were eager to strike back.

The third point is more subtle. Most versions of chaos magic teach that gods and spirits are simply hypersigils devised and empowered by old religious and magical traditions, rather than conscious nonphysical beings with their own intentions and powers. Many chaos mages, in fact, like to treat the universe as a blank slate in which human beings are the only active presences. As a result, very few chaos mages learn how to work safely with gods and spirits who aren't the products of human minds. That's something that traditional occultists know how to do, and it informs many of the basic practices and teachings of traditional occultism, but these protections were among the things that the early chaos mages discarded when they broke with traditional occultism.

As a result, some thousands of young and angry outcasts who were part of the chans and a galaxy of similar online communities took up the intensive study and practice of basic magical workings without any sense of how to manage interactions with nonphysical beings—or, indeed, any notion that such interactions might need to be managed. That, in turn, pretty much guaranteed that if something other than human took an interest in the situation, a lot of the graduates of the chans' magical boot camps were going to be swept up in something over which they had no control at all. The shortest description of 2016 is that that's what happened.

To make sense of what followed, it's going to be necessary to take a closer look at a corner of internet culture that most of my readers have probably never encountered in person: the online forums known collectively as "the chans." These started out innocuously enough with Futaba Channel, a Japanese-language electronic meeting place for fans of anime, which (for reasons that make perfect sense if you speak Japanese) came to be called "2chan" in online slang. In 2003, in much the same way that an amoeba breeds, a group of anime fans hived off onto a new site, 4chan, which did the same thing in the English language.

In the same way, other sites such as 8chan spun off 4chan in due time. In practice, 4chan and all its offspring are venues for anonymous unmoderated talk, places where anything goes—the more offensive to the conventional wisdom, the better. Long before Trump announced his candidacy, the chans were already having a significant impact on internet culture. Most people these days know, for example, what a lolcat is; 4chan *invented* lolcats. One of the subdivisions of 4chan and many of its offshoots is /pol/, short for "politically incorrect," and that's one of the places where the young and disgruntled gathered to talk about the things you can't talk about in the workplace or the academy these days.

That's a phenomenon that deserves a little further discussion here. One of the lessons of the history of morals is that the more stridently you repress something, the more desperately people want to do it. The status of sex in the Victorian period is an example we've already discussed. The drug abuse epidemic in the United States today, similarly, is almost entirely a product of the much-ballyhooed War on Drugs—countries that treat drug addiction as an ordinary medical issue, not a subject for moral grandstanding, have much lower rates of drug use.

Recent crusades against "hate speech" have had exactly the same effect in today's America. Those who attend university classes or work in white-collar jobs know that their every word is scrutinized by jealous rivals ready to use accusations of sexism, racism, or the like as a weapon in the endless competition for status. Many people, forced into so stifling an environment, will end up desperately longing for a place where they can take a deep breath and say absolutely anything, no matter how offensive. The chans were among the internet venues that offered them that freedom. Posts on the chans are anonymous, so there was no risk of reprisal, and the culture of the chans (and especially of /pol/) tends to applaud extreme statements, so they became a magnet for the people who for one reason or another lost out in the struggle to become flunkeys of the established order of society, were locked out of what had been the normal trajectory of adult independence by plunging wages and soaring rents, and were incensed by the smug superiority of a system that assumed that it had all the answers.

It's become pretty much de rigueur among the respectable to denounce the chans as racist, sexist, and anti-Semitic. Is there racism, sexism, and anti-Semitism in /pol/ and its many equivalents? You bet, but that's far from the whole story. A venue that allows people to say anything anonymously is going to field whatever kinds of speech are most loudly forbidden. What was going on in the chans was considerably broader than those categories suggest: every value, every bias, every presupposition of the cultural mainstream was being shouted down with maximum glee. That's what you get in outsider culture.

You also get running jokes, odd mascots, and odd little bits of in-group slang. That's where Pepe the Frog came in. He started out in 2005 as a character in Matt Furie's comic strip *Boy's Club,* an archetypal slacker who just didn't care about anything. He got splashed across the internet in the usual fashion, and ended up being adopted by /pol/ as its mascot. Then there was the word *kek,* which is what you get due to a software oddity when you try to send the message LOL to one of the factions in the online *World of Warcraft* game. In the chans, "kek" became the sound of laughter—which oddly enough is what the word means in Korean.

There's one more detail of chan culture you need to know to follow what happened. I mentioned that posts on the chans are anonymous. What identifies each post is that it gets assigned a sequential number by the board software. The poster has no way of knowing what the number will be until the post goes up, and it became first a running joke and then a minor obsession to look for repeated digits—say, the 333 in 14186333. A doubled digit is a "dub," a tripled digit a "trip," and so on. Any repeating digit is a "get."

The moment Donald Trump declared his candidacy, a significant number of /pol/ participants rallied to his cause. It was a match made in—well, probably not heaven, but you get the point: Trump's bombastic brashness and the sheer parodic potential of a reality TV star running for U.S. president made him an instant favorite on /pol/, and so did his loud rejection of the conventional wisdom of U.S. politics. There Was No Alternative until Trump offered one, calling for a massive pruning of Federal regulation, a rejection of free-trade ideology, and an end to the tacit encouragement of illegal immigration: the elimination, that is, of the three core elements of the policies that crushed the American wage class. For obvious reasons, all this went over extremely well in the venues we're discussing.

Trump's candidacy had another attraction to /pol/, though. It succeeded, deliberately or by accident, in teaching the alt-right a lesson that provided the basement brigade with an endless supply of keks, which is that salary-class liberals and the media that serve them can very easily be goaded into self-defeating overreactions. One example out of many is the exquisitely clever alt-right strategy of posting signs saying IT'S OKAY TO BE WHITE all over college campuses. The standard liberal reaction to this is a fine spluttering meltdown, in which this inoffensive utterance is denounced as hate speech that must be punished.

From within the American Left, no doubt such meltdowns look like a proper display of moral virtue. From any other perspective, they look like an admission that the entire social justice movement is motivated by nothing better than bigotry against white people, and that the salary class is therefore no better than the ordinary deplorable Americans it loves to hate. So the basement dwellers plunged gleefully into the fray, turning out wickedly funny pro-Trump internet memes and getting the left to give the memes plenty of free publicity in the form of frenzied denunciations. Somewhere in this process, though, people on /pol/ started noticing that posts referencing Trump were fielding an unusually high number of "gets."

By this time some of the Trump supporters on /pol/ were learning chaos magic and putting it to work on behalf of their candidate. Memes putting Trump's hair on Pepe the Frog, setting Trump and Pepe side by side as running mates, or involving Pepe in the Trump campaign in other ways, were blossoming all over the chans and spreading out into the rest of the internet. Loud kekking arose as pro-Trump posts fielded "get" after "get"—and then June 19, 2016, came around, and some anonymous user on 4chan typed in "Trump will win" in response to a long string of irrelevant posts, and hit the enter button.

That turned out to be post number 77777777.

It was somewhere around this same time, too, that someone on the chans noticed that "kek" wasn't just a funny way of saying LOL. It was also the name of an ancient Egyptian god, a deity of the primeval darkness that gave birth to the light, who was worshiped in the city of Hermopolis—and who was very often portrayed as an anthropomorphic frog like Pepe. Following up this clue, another anonymous user found on the internet the photo of an ancient Egyptian statue of a frog, mislabeled as a statue of Kek. It was actually a statue of the frog goddess Heqet, but no one realized that at first—and to a modern eye, the hieroglyphics of the name Heqet look unnervingly like a person sitting in front of a computer screen, with a swirling shape like magical energies on the far side of the screen.

By the time this finished percolating through the chans, a great many people in that corner of the internet were convinced, or ironically pretended to be convinced, and at all events acted as though they were convinced, that Donald Trump was the anointed candidate of the god Kek, bringer of daylight, who had manifested as Pepe the Frog and was communicating his approval to them with "gets." In response, the chaos mages of /pol/ flung themselves even more passionately into action. Those of my readers who followed the 2016 U.S. election will remember that rumors were swirling around the Democratic candidate Hillary Clinton by late summer of that year, claiming that she had a debilitating health condition that she was hiding from the media and the voters. The operative mages on /pol/ focused their efforts on a single goal: making Hillary Clinton collapse in public.

September 11, 2016, duly came, and on that day three things happened. First, Clinton publicly denounced Pepe the Frog as a right-wing hate symbol, to the great delight of the chans—all that free publicity for their mascot! Then, as she left a memorial service for the World Trade Center attacks, in view of the cameras, she swayed, toppled, and had to be hauled into her waiting SUV like a side of beef. The GOP rumor mill went wild, and the chaos mages of /pol/ did the digital equivalent of looking at each other in shock. There's a useful acronym in occult circles, TSW—the polite version of its meaning is "this stuff works"—and everyone who's ever taught magic to novices is used to the inevitable TSW panic, the vertiginous moment at which the student finally grasps that there's more to magic than make-believe, and usually has to be talked down from a state close to hysteria. The chans went through their own TSW moment that day.

Then there was the third event the same day. Yet another anonymous poster stumbled on a piece of Europop music from the 1980s, a forgettable song titled "Shadilay." The record label had a cartoon frog on it, waving a magic wand. The band's name? P.E.P.E. This hit the chans the same day that Hillary Clinton denounced Pepe the Frog and took a tumble. Many people on the chans decided, or ironically pretended to have decided, and at all events acted as though they had decided, that they'd just received a big vote of confidence from Kek the Frog God.

The song "Shadilay" duly became /pol/'s anthem, and the word "Shadilay!" itself took on the same status for Kek's faithful that "Allahu Akbar!" has among devout Muslims. After that, if Donald Trump had called on his supporters on the chans to walk into the sea, there's a fair chance they would have done it—and the chaos mages on /pol/ and its equivalents rallied around the banner of the Frog God with frantic intensity, flooding the internet with memes, as the campaign entered its crucial weeks, and kept up that intensity straight through Election Day.

I know this is unacceptable to suggest this in most corners of today's industrial culture, but it's worth considering the possibility that the efforts of /pol/'s chaos mages might have had something to do with the unexpected outcome of the 2016 election. As occultists like to say, TSW, and it really doesn't matter whether or not currently popular notions about the world provide a theory to explain the efficacy of magic. Every human society around the planet and throughout time has practiced magic, and the most parsimonious explanation for that fact is that the art and science of causing changes in consciousness in accordance with will really can cause changes in consciousness in accordance with will.

In the consciousness of a great many Americans, certainly, attitudes toward Donald Trump shifted in the last weeks before the election from "What a pompous blowhard!" to "Yeah, he's a pompous blowhard, but if he wins, things might improve for me and my family." Such thoughts, spreading through the crawlspaces of the collective conversation of our time, had a great deal to do with Trump's victory—and magic may have been part of what put them there.

The aftermath of that victory saw the alt-right riding high. After the chans got over their shock and delight, many of the same chaos mages who'd worked overtime to make that happen decided to use the same techniques to further similar projects. More magical workings, calling on Kek through his manifestation as Pepe the Frog, got launched for the next project: winning the upcoming French presidential election for Front National candidate Marine Le Pen. She lost. Several similar projects were launched and heavily backed by /pol/ chaos mages, and they failed just as badly. As far as I know, none of these other projects were answered by torrents of "gets" and cascades of meaningful coincidences.

Nor did those signs show up during Trump's reelection campaign in 2020. To my mind, this is among the most crucial details of the magical side of the Trump phenomenon. The high strangeness on both sides of the 2016 campaign did not recur, and so what happened instead was a brutal but ordinary political campaign pitting two controversial and widely disliked politicians against one another. Both sides went into the fray expecting to sweep the field, and for all practical purposes, both sides lost.

Why that happened, and what it reveals about the deeper dimensions of the magical politics of our time, will occupy chapter six of this work. Before we plunge into the depths, however, it's necessary to look at the magic on the other side—for the alt-right chaos mages had their exact equivalents on the other side of the political spectrum. Their part in the magical side of the age of Trump also deserves examination.

5

The Court of the Dragon

The Magic Resistance, the Shadow, and the Changer

Then I drew on the white silk robe, embroidered with the Yellow Sign, and placed the crown on my head. At last I was King, King by my right in Hastur, King because I knew the mystery of the Hyades, and my mind had sounded the depths of the Lake of Hali. I was King! The first gray penciling of dawn would raise a tempest that would shake two hemispheres. Then as I stood, my every nerve pitched to the highest tension, faint with the joy and splendour of my thought, without, in the dark passage, a man groaned.

FROM "THE REPAIRER OF REPUTATIONS"

IN *THE KING IN YELLOW*

One of the more interesting ironies of the role of magic in the rise of Trump is that his opponents were so much better prepared to use magic than his supporters. The liberal slant of the Theosophical Society mentioned early in the previous chapter was a harbinger of trends in the politics of American magic that have remained in place ever since. While there have always been some conservatives in the alternative spirituality scene across the Western world, they have been a minority from the late nineteenth century to the present. In the United States—matters are different in some other countries—political conservatism has long been linked with traditional religious views or with certain kinds of atheism, while the most popular alternative spiritualities from Theosophy to Wicca have close and longstanding ties with liberal political beliefs.

In 2016, certainly, the largest and most visibly active alternative-spirituality movements in America were explicitly aligned with the Democratic Party. Wicca and most other Neopagan traditions were solidly in the Democratic camp; so was the feminist Goddess spirituality scene, which partly overlaps with Wicca; so was most of the American Buddhist community. So, crucially, were large majorities in the broad penumbra of American alternative spirituality, far larger than any of these, in which the detritus of more than three hundred years of spiritual pop culture bobs around like the apples American children used to duck for every Halloween. Many of the people in these varied scenes had at least some training in magic, and some knew a great deal about the subject. The obvious question is why they didn't bring their abilities to bear on the election.

The answer is that they didn't think they needed to do anything at all. One of the things that made the outcome of the election such a blow to Democrats was that next to no one on their side of the political landscape thought that Donald Trump had any chance of victory. Like so many of their fellow Democrats, the people who might have organized magical workings to keep Trump from winning went to election night parties on November 3 in the serene conviction that Hillary Clinton was certain to become the next president of the United States.

It took a few months after the election for what came to call itself the Magic Resistance to begin to get organized. Once it finally sank in that Donald Trump really was moving into the White House, though, the first magical workings to unseat him and frustrate his agenda got under way. Their efforts were easy enough to track. Where the chaos mages of the alt-right planned their workings on obscure message boards on the fringes of the internet, or took things entirely private, the Magic Resistance splashed theirs over high-traffic websites such as Medium.com, blogged about them incessantly, and filled several books with detailed accounts of the workings they were using. One consequence of this increased publicity was that the workings aimed at stopping Trump were carried out and supported by many more people than those that helped put him into office; exact totals are difficult to measure in either case, but it seems likely that the early workings of the Magic Resistance had something like an order of magnitude more participants than the magical workings of the chans.

Magic is not always on the side of the largest battalions, however. The results of the workings planned and carried out by the Magic Resistance ranged from inconclusive to total failure. The most successful of their workings, the Blue Wave spell meant to bring about a comprehensive Democratic victory in the 2018 midterm election, may have contributed to the Democratic takeover of the House of Representatives—though a swing back to the party out of power is of course a standard feature of midterm elections. The same election, however, saw the Republican majority in the Senate increase by a crucial handful of seats, enough to guarantee that attempts to impeach Trump or stop him from appointing conservative judges to the Federal courts would go nowhere.

The other end of the scale was measured by the all-out effort the Magic Resistance launched in 2018 to stop Brett Kavanaugh from being confirmed as a Supreme Court justice. When Kavanaugh's nomination went to the Senate, the GOP still had only a razor-thin 51–49 majority in that body, and there was a real chance that Democratic efforts to sink the nomination would succeed. The day after the Magic Resistance working was splashed over the internet—again, it appeared on Medium.com— the senatorial resistance to Kavanaugh's candidacy suddenly collapsed, and he was confirmed and sworn in without further incident.

That was the Gettysburg of the Magic Resistance. After it, for the most part, further attempts to stop Trump by magical means went on in private if they went on at all. That changed briefly in 2020, when a last burst of public rituals aimed at deposing Trump were carried out with maximum publicity, and once again the Blue Wave the rituals attempted to set in motion failed to show up, leaving Congress even more bitterly divided than it had been and the presidency held hostage to recounts and lawsuits.

Why did the Magic Resistance fail so completely when the alt-right succeeded? To understand that it's necessary to plunge deeper into the tactics of magic and the way that magic intertwines with political power in today's America.

An earlier chapter (pp. 90–107) explored at some length the magic of the excluded, but it's also crucial to understand the other side of the equation, the magic of the excluders. The necessity for this dimension of magic rises in proportion to the gap between an aristocracy's self-image and the consequences of its rule. The system of doublethink discussed earlier in this book, which demanded support for policies that devastated America's working class but forbade any mention of the consequences of those policies, is a classic example of that process at work. Central to the self-image of the salary class in the United States, as elsewhere in the industrial world, is the serene conviction that they are the Good People, leading the march of progress toward better things for everyone who matters—and this belief not merely persisted but became more and more essential as the human cost of the status quo mounted steadily upward.

The unspeakable truth that shaped the discourse of the pre-Trump era was that the Good People, the morally virtuous people, enthusiastically supported policies that plunged tens of millions of Americans into poverty and misery. In the usual fashion of aristocracies, the Good People insisted that the policies that benefited them were the only morally thinkable options, and that anyone who objected to them could only be motivated by deliberate evil. For those inside the self-referential bubble of elite culture, it all seemed so straightforward: the sufferings of those people whose interests aligned with those of the privileged were all-important and had to be addressed, while the sufferings of those who were being crushed by policies that benefited the privileged were their own fault and didn't matter anyway.

This sort of thinking doesn't come easily. Sustaining it takes, in fact, a fairly systematic use of the art and science of causing changes in consciousness in accordance with will. That's why, while people outside the privileged classes made the last forty years one of the golden ages of popular occultism (and helped to pay my rent with their book purchases), people within the privileged classes were embracing their own varieties of magic. It's why Fortune 500 corporations encouraged their high-end employees to take up mindfulness meditation and various other bits of mildly exotic spiritual practice that had been carefully stripped of all their original moral and religious content. It's why a great deal of similarly sanitized spirituality found its way into general circulation among the well-to-do.

Some cultural critics have dismissed these things as a slightly less chemical form of tranquilizer, and while there's a good sharp point to that jab, it's not the whole story. The magic of the excluders exists to convince its practitioners that nothing can possibly be wrong with the world, that everything is as it should be, and that any remaining problems can be counted on to go away in good time once the right reforms get put into place and the right people get elected. It's a tool that assists the comfortable to stay comfortable by excluding unwelcome realities.

Here again, though, the magic of the excluders becomes more popular as the number of unwelcome realities to exclude goes up. That happens, in turn, when the number of people whose needs and grievances aren't being addressed by the existing political order goes up. Thus a society in the face of certain kinds of crisis experiences a double upsurge in magic: among the underprivileged, as a way of changing things, and among the overprivileged, as a way of hiding from the need to change things.

It is in this way that societies fissure into the excluded and the excluders, and each of these separate and unequal halves turn to magic: the excluded to seek change, the excluders to convince themselves that there's no need for change. Under most circumstances these paired magical intentions find a relatively stable balance. The aristocracy bumbles along merrily in its self-referential bubble, convinced that truth and decency are on its side and all is right with the world. Meanwhile, outside the bubble, those who are blocked from using more ordinary means to pursue their needs and wants or seek redress for their grievances apply magic on a case-by-case basis to improve their own lives.

That's business as usual in a society in which the privileged classes have convinced themselves that There Is No Alternative to a set of policies that benefit them at everyone else's expense. It becomes business as *un*usual once the mistake mentioned earlier—the habit of educating far more people for managerial jobs than there are jobs to employ them—builds a large enough intellectual underclass of young people who have plenty of skills and no prospects for the future, and who turn to one of the available strategies to try to overturn the system.

It's at this point that the magic of the excluders can turn into a disastrous liability. It's quite easy to use the fashionable magic of the privileged to make yourself completely oblivious to what's happening right under your nose. This becomes all the more tempting as the risks of ignoring what's happening become more severe.

Examples? Here's Charles I of England, who used the Hermeticism of the late Renaissance and a good solid dose of establishment Christianity to blind himself to the way that his policies were leading his country straight into a civil war he couldn't win and didn't survive. Here's Nicholas II, Tsar of All the Russias, using the mystical end of Russian Orthodox spirituality to back himself into exactly the same corner with exactly the same gory results. Here's Adolf Hitler, using the pop occultism he learned in his Vienna days to convince himself and his inner circle that he couldn't possibly lose, and losing all the more catastrophically as a result. There are plenty of others of the same type.

In 2016, Hillary Clinton followed that same well-trodden path. While Trump worked hard to win the election, crisscrossing the country from one rally to another in a highly successful effort to do an end run around the mainstream media and get his message directly to the voters, it's fair to say that his path to the White House was made far easier by Clinton's stunningly inept campaign.

Some of that ineptitude was pretty clearly Clinton's own doing. It's indicative, for example, that her 2016 campaign was all but identical to her failed run in 2008. The only reason that she didn't suffer an identical defeat in the primaries, with Bernie Sanders reprising the role played by Barack Obama in the earlier campaign, is that Clinton made sure to get the party apparatchiks on her side, and they bent, broke, and trampled the rules to hand her the nomination. Of course that move ended up costing her dearly in the general election, as millions of Democratic voters stayed home rather than cast a vote for a candidate they felt had cheated her way to the nomination, but that kind of own goal was par for the course in her campaign.

Still, the thing that doomed Clinton's campaign, more than anything else, was the inability of the candidate and her inner circle of advisers and managers to notice that anything was going wrong. Every time polls showed that a very large percentage of American voters disliked and distrusted their candidate, Clinton's handlers simply looked blank and set out to reintroduce her to the voters, and when that didn't work—and it never did—they simply looked blank and tried again. It really did look as though they were under a spell.

As the 2016 campaign wore on, the Clinton machine's detachment from reality became even more pronounced. People who were involved in the Clinton campaign have written about the way their increasingly desperate attempts to warn the national leadership that Trump was gaining ground in crucial swing states were brushed aside as irrelevant, while millions of dollars were wasted on venues such as Chicago, which the Democrats would have won easily if they'd nominated Zippy the Pinhead. As Trump held rally after rally in the swing states of the upper Midwest, and the numbers shifted further his way with every poll, the Clinton campaign ignored those battleground states and lumbered ahead as though going through the right motions would conjure up the victory that they seemed to think the universe owed them.

I'd be interested to know, if anyone kept such statistics, how many people in Clinton's campaign staff practiced the watered-down versions of mindfulness meditation, yoga, and similar practices that make up so large a part of the magic of the privileged in today's America. The central problem with such practices, when they've been pried loose from their original context and the challenging connections to spiritual realities those include, is that they become very effective at convincing you that everything is wonderful, even when it's critical to realize that everything *isn't* wonderful and drastic action has to be taken right away to avert catastrophe. Such anecdotal evidence as I've heard suggests that such practices were at least as widespread among Clinton campaign staff as they are in affluent liberal circles generally, and may have been considerably more so. If that's the case, by leading her staff to ignore the signs of impending disaster, they may have played a crucial role in costing Clinton the election.

After the election, in turn, the same weird paralysis that seized the Clinton campaign remained frozen in place among her supporters, and more generally among Trump's opponents. To some extent, this is simply a function of the magic of the excluders we've already discussed. Members of the salary class very rarely stray out of their bubbles of privilege to encounter the rest of America and find out what's happening there, and so it's easy for them to convince themselves that everything is for the best in this best of all possible worlds. Add a collection of spiritual practices reworked so that they function to keep one's attention limited as strictly as possible to one's own comfortable surroundings, and a state of detachment bordering on florid delusion is not out of reach.

✳

In 2016 such techniques were readily available to the Clinton campaign, and to everyone else who wanted to retreat into some such state of delusion. The positive thinking movement of the late twentieth and early twenty-first centuries had that to its credit. In her book *Bright-Sided,* which should be required reading for anyone who hopes to understand the 2016 and 2020 elections, Barbara Ehrenreich did a fair job of sketching out the rise of positive thinking to its current status as a cultural norm in today's elite American subcultures. As with most of her books, the sound of grinding axes is always audible through her prose, but it is worth putting up with that to see what she notices—and also what she misses.

It's a fascinating story. What used to be called "New Thought," back when it was actually new, was set in motion by Phineas Parkhurst Quimby, the son of a dirt-poor New Hampshire farmer who became interested in Mesmerism, the stranger and more interesting ancestor of modern hypnotism. Sometime in the 1850s he became convinced that what made his treatments work was not the subtle energy that Mesmer called animal magnetism, but the attitude of his patients, and he began to give his patients pep talks instead of Mesmeric treatments, with very good results. From him, by way of a chain of events in which Christian Science founder Mary Baker Eddy played a significant role, the New Thought movement got started.

New Thought has been a significant force in American culture ever since. One of the details that Ehrenreich missed is that over the century or so that followed its creation, New Thought diverged into two currents, which we can call the pragmatic and the megalomaniac wings of the movement. The pragmatic wing was typified by figures such as Rev. Norman Vincent Peale, among the most popular self-help authors of the middle years of the twentieth century. Pragmatic New Thought by and large makes no supernatural claims; it simply points out that many people keep themselves from succeeding by their own lack of confidence and enthusiasm, and offers ways to overcome those barriers. Its popularity is understandable, because it very often works—within reason. You don't accomplish miracles by the methods of the pragmatic wing of New Thought. You simply face life with confidence and enthusiasm instead of dread and self-doubt, and tolerably often you get better results.

Then there's the megalomaniac wing. Most of the books that were central to that end of New Thought back in the day have long since been forgotten, but fortunately we have a fine example of the species in Rhonda Byrne's brilliantly marketed 2006 book and DVD *The Secret.* The secret in Byrne's book is of course the so-called Law of Attraction, which is basically the claim that if you want something bad enough the universe is obliged to give it to you. Byrne's philosophy thus might best be described as a sense of entitlement inflated to cosmic scale.

It also doesn't work. When *The Secret* was first published, I lived in Ashland, Oregon, which at the time had a higher concentration of New Age believers per capita than any other town north of the California border, and I knew a good many people who bought the book and immediately set out to use it to get rich flipping houses in the booming real estate market of that time. All of them ended up taking heavy losses when the market turned south in 2008, and most had to declare bankruptcy. More generally, *The Secret* sold millions of copies in its first year or so but had sales fall off fairly steeply thereafter, because the mere fact you can convince yourself of something does not make the universe play along.

In *Bright-Sided,* Barbara Ehrenreich focused her attention almost exclusively on the megalomaniac wing of the positive-thinking movement, since this suited her polemic purpose better than the quieter and more productive pragmatic wing. By doing this, ironically, the author of *Nickel and Dimed*—one of the best descriptions of the predicament of the wage class in today's America—missed her chance to observe the massive role that social class and expectations play in the functions and dysfunctions of positive thinking.

When Phineas Parkhurst Quimby introduced the gospel of positive thinking, most of his patients were middle-class women. At that time, in the middle years of the Victorian era, women of the respectable classes were saddled with ideologies that glorified feminine helplessness. As Bram Dijkstra chronicles in *Idols of Perversity,* his useful history of Victorian attitudes toward women, the cult of the female invalid was in full swing just then, and imposed a severe psychological burden on many women. Quimby's calm insistence that his patients really could get up and do something with their lives thus had a revolutionary effect. The same thing was just as true as New Thought spread out of its original settings and became, among other things, a major theme in the self-help literature of the late nineteenth- and early twentieth-century African American community. To those who have been told over and over again that they can't accomplish anything, the positive-thinking gospel can be a revelation, not to mention a source of considerable success in life.

One man's meat is another man's poison, however, and when positive thinking found its way into social classes that were used to getting whatever they wanted, the results were disastrous. A set of ideas that balances out the negative programming that the underprivileged have received all their lives can become a source of severe imbalance once it reaches people who already believe that they ought to get whatever they want—and this belief, after all, is normal for the overprivileged classes of every society. That was what turned Quimby's practical pep talks into the cosmically overinflated sense of entitlement marketed so efficiently by Rhonda Byrne. It was also very likely one of the core factors that led Hillary Clinton's campaign to believe media polls that systematically oversampled Democratic voters to produce the illusion of inevitable victory, and kept her and her strategists from realizing that things were going wrong until it was far too late to do anything about it.

One further irony, and it's a rich one, is that Donald Trump was also profoundly influenced by the positive-thinking gospel. The church he attended as a boy and young man, the church where he married his first wife, was presided over by none other than Rev. Norman Vincent Peale of *The Power of Positive Thinking* fame. Read Trump's published statements and it's impossible to miss the presence of New Thought ideas all through them. Those ideas are inevitably drawn from the pragmatic wing of the movement. No Law of Attraction governs his words and actions, just unflagging enthusiasm and limitless self-confidence. That helped him immensely at various points of his career, but it may well have been responsible for the overconfidence that helped make the 2020 election the bipartisan debacle that it became.

The history of New Thought helped frame the background against which the Magic Resistance emerged, and it helps explain one of the more intriguing things about the Left's sudden turn to magic after the 2016 election. This is the fact that the turn in question wasn't limited in its appeal to those Democratic voters who practiced Neopagan spirituality or had some other existing connection to magical practices. While Neopagans were well represented in the Magic Resistance, a great many people got involved in it who had no prior interest or involvement in magic at all. That shows among other things just how deeply Trump's election shook the confidence of the salary class, since before 2016 claims of superior rationality had been an important part of the self-image of the salary class in America.

Now of course a crisis of confidence could have done the American salary class a great deal of good just then. If Trump's election had forced its members to reconsider their approach to politics and society, and to accept the possibility that the needs and opinions of the wage class might be a significant concern of public policy, the Democratic party might have been able to learn the lessons of its defeat, return to the electorate with a platform better suited to attract support from undecided voters, and sweep the 2020 election. Instead, a great many of them made the opposite choice—a choice that gets made constantly on a more personal level.

If you're an operative mage and you allow your magical work to become a matter of public knowledge, you can count on receiving a variety of inquiries. One of the most common is also one of the saddest and most futile. These come from people who have backed themselves into a corner, and want you to use magic to help them avoid the consequences. The nature of the corner they've backed into varies across the whole vast spectrum of human folly, but in every case the root of the trouble is the self-defeating conviction that they ought to be able to keep on doing the same thing over and over again, and get different results.

What's more, people who come to operative mages with pleas of this kind inevitably turn to magic only after every other option has failed. You know you've got a case of this kind when the person enumerates all the things he or she has done to deal with the problem (or rather, in nearly every case, to avoid dealing with the problem) before coming to you for help. It's almost never possible to do anything useful for such people, partly because magic is most effective early in any situation when changes in consciousness can have the most effect, and partly because the one thing that might help—getting them to change whatever it is they are doing that is causing the problem—is the one thing that you can be sure they'll never be willing to do.

An equivalent set of attitudes could be seen all through the Magic Resistance as it started its campaign to use magic to unseat the Trump administration. Perhaps the clearest expression of that self-defeating approach was the insistence on the part of the movement's public figureheads that three of the core rules of magical practice didn't apply to them. Every competently trained mage knows that effective magic requires unity of intention. Every competently trained mage knows that effective magic requires what military personnel like to call OPSEC; for the rest of us, that's operational security, better known as keeping your mouth shut. Every competently trained mage also knows that it's much more effective to build your side up than to tear the other side down. The Magic Resistance did none of these things. What's more, when these issues came up for discussion—and they did, all over the ends of the internet where occultists talk—leading figures of the Magic Resistance insisted angrily that neither of these three rules were valid and their magic was certain to triumph anyway.

It's worth taking a closer look at each of the rules in question, to understand how this affected the outcome. Unity of intention is necessary in magical practice because the ability of human beings to cause changes in consciousness in accordance with will is far from limitless. For the same reason that you can't power all the electric appliances in your home with a single nine-volt battery, you can't cause a large number of significant changes in consciousness all at once with a single magical working, and this is especially true when the people you're trying to affect are pushing in the opposite direction, with or without the help of magical techniques.

The magical workings of the alt-right had the effects they did because so many of those workings focused with laser intensity on one task at a time, using one hypersigil at a time, with a single appropriate symbolic pattern at its heart. The workings of the Magic Resistance, by contrast, went out of their way to avoid doing any of these things. Read the rituals in *Magic for the Resistance* by Michael M. Hughes, for example—that was the most popular of the books mentioned above— and in most of them you'll find a laundry list of intentions, a gallimaufry of incoherent symbolism, and a set of ritual actions with no particular relation to one another. This does not make for effective magic.

Perhaps the extreme example of this habit was a lavishly advertised working in 2018, at a Wiccan bookstore in Brooklyn. Participants were encouraged to bring to the event lists of everything they were upset about, so that all those things could be included in the working's intention! The official purpose of the working was to stop Brett Kavanaugh from being confirmed as a Supreme Court justice. I noted at the time on my online journal that Kavanaugh had nothing to worry about— and of course he didn't.

The failure to establish a single focus of intention and stick with it might have doomed the Magic Resistance all by itself. Far more problematic, however, was the movement's flat refusal to maintain basic operational security around their workings. That's a critical issue in magic, and one that's very well known among operative mages. Back in 1854, when Eliphas Lévi kicked the modern magical revival into gear with his bestselling *Doctrine and Ritual of High Magic,* he set out the four basic rules of magical practice; to know, to dare, to will, and to be silent. (One of my teachers used to finish up this quartet of principles with "... and to shut the fuck up!") That last rule has been tested and worked out in detail by generations of operative mages, and it works: if you keep your workings private, you get better results than if you discuss them with those who are not actively involved in them.

At least two distinct processes make this rule important for the operative mage. To begin with, magic is among other things a creative art, distinct from most other arts in that the artist and the audience are the same person. Most of us have encountered would-be writers who talk endlessly about the novels they're going to write and so inevitably never get around to writing them. Every other art has its equivalent examples—those who have never quite gotten around to noticing that talking about creative projects is a fine way to disperse the energy that might otherwise make them happen. Conversely, most successful writers, poets, painters, and other artists know how important it is to keep their mouths shut during the crucial stages of the creative process. Magic is no different.

Yet there's another reason to keep your mouth shut whenever your magic is in conflict with someone else's. If you're playing poker and the other players know what cards you've got in your hand, you lose. If you're the Allies and you're about to launch the D-Day invasion into occupied France, and the German high command knows in advance where your landing zones are, once again, you lose. Magic is not exempt from this same principle. If you intend to achieve something using magic and other people who know how to use magic want to stop you from achieving it, letting them know the details of your rituals is a good way to get clobbered.

Rituals, to shift metaphors, are delicate machineries, and a mon-

key wrench dropped into the gears in the right place can do an effi-
cient job of jamming them up. Exactly how a given ritual can best be
monkeywrenched varies depending on the details of the ritual. As a
rule, however, the more unity of intention a ritual has, the more tautly
focused its symbolism is, and the more coherent are the actions that
compose it, the harder hostile mages have to work if they want to mess
with it. The reverse, of course, is equally true—and the workings of
the Magic Resistance accordingly became a target-rich environment for
those mages on the other side of the Kek Wars who decided to play
hob with their opponent's workings. How much of the failure of the
Magic Resistance came from those counter-workings is a difficult question to answer, but the likelihood that they played a significant role is
not small.

Finally, there's the issue of building up your side rather than tearing
down the other side. The entire subject of magical ethics is contested
territory these days, but we can stay clear of that by focusing on the
simpler question of what works. Here Dion Fortune is again a knowledgeable guide. In the early years of the Second World War she organized a massive magical working aimed at keeping Britain out of the
hands of the Nazis, and the letters that coordinated the effort have been
published as *The Magical Battle of Britain*—a book that deserves close
attention from anyone interested in the practice of political magic. Her
rule throughout the working was to focus on strengthening the collective consciousness of Britain and the Allies, and she dismissed the suggestion that the working should attempt to harm the Nazis with words
that today's political activists on both sides might take to heart: "Hate
is an evil thing in itself, whatever its provocation, and to call it righ-
teous indignation does little to improve it" (Fortune 1993, 11).

Such points are routinely dismissed by the belligerently minded
as so much pacifistic poppycock. It bears remembering, though, that
the Nazi government against which Britain was contending just then
included a great many people with occult training—Adolf Hitler,
Heinrich Himmler, and Rudolf Hess among them—and an ideology

that glorified hatred. The details of their magical workings did not survive the demolition of the SS ritual center at Wewelsburg just before the war ended, but given the ideas expressed by Hitler et al., those workings certainly aimed at destroying Germany's enemies. Notice which of these contending sorceries won.

None of this should have been news to those participants who came to the Magic Resistance with previous training and experience in magic. Read the standard textbooks of magical training in circulation in the decades immediately before 2016 and you can find each of the points I've made, often elaborated in much more detail than I've given them here. Why all those basic points of magical instruction went out the window when the Magic Resistance began to organize its efforts is a fascinating question, and will lead us another step deeper into the magical dimensions of the Trump phenomenon.

To begin with, one of the main reasons why the Magic Resistance threw aside unity of intention, operational security, and a positive focus to their workings is that all these things would have made it much more difficult to engage in virtue signaling. As we have discussed in earlier chapters, virtue signaling is not a casual thing in a society like ours. It's one of the essential ways by which those who hope to become flunkeys in the service of the existing order of society try to attract favorable attention. Participation in the Magic Resistance was tailor-made for this sort of symbolic display, so long as the workings the movement organized were public, highly visible, and addressed as wide a range of virtue signals as possible. That these considerations made those workings ineffective for their ostensible purpose hardly mattered. Plenty of other projects encouraged by the salary class, including most of the measures supposedly meant to help the wage and welfare classes, can be understood in the same way.

Yet there was more at work in the failure of the Magic Resistance than this. Another important reason for that failure is the belief, pervasive all across the leftward end of American politics, that history has an inherent tilt toward improvement—and more to the point, toward the kinds of improvement that benefit the privileged classes of today's society. Hillary Clinton, in an impromptu response to a heckler at one of her campaign appearances, phrased the central tenet of that faith concisely: "We're not going to go back. We're going to go forward." Like Clinton herself, a great many of her followers saw their cause as another step forward in the inevitable march of social progress, and to find themselves "going back" is profoundly disorienting—even though those labels "forward" and "back" have been assigned for crassly political reasons.

Once again, however, there's clearly more going on here than either of these two factors can explain. Day after day, Trump's opponents staged shrill but politically ineffective meltdowns over whatever Trump happened to have said or done most recently, as though cries of outrage counted as effective political action. Trump very quickly learned to use the effect for his own purposes—deliberately saying and doing things to send his opponents into a swivet, so that they don't notice that his administration was doing something else on another subject that his opponents would protest if they weren't too busy shrieking to notice.

Day after day, for that matter, the movers and shakers of the Democratic Party aligned themselves with a set of policies that are supported by a small fraction of the electorate and rejected by the rest. When the candidates at one of the Democratic debates early in 2020 were asked whether they supported free health care for illegal immigrants, and every one of them raised a hand, they drew a hard line between their party and most of the U.S. electorate. When Democratic politicians refused to acknowledge the looting and arson of the 2020 riots and spoke only of "peaceful protesters," they did the same thing. There are plenty of other examples. Political parties that want to win big in elections don't veer toward extreme positions and insist that the voters have to follow them there.

All the while, anyone who suggested the two crucial actions that could have won the next election for the Democrats—first, figuring out what cost them the 2016 election so they can stop doing it; and second, finding ways to win back the loyalty of the normally Democratic wage-class voters who stayed home or voted for Trump in 2016, after having been ignored by the Democratic Party once too often—got shouted down. Instead, Trump's opponents just kept doubling down on the same mistakes that put Trump in the White House. It's as though they lost the capacity not only to learn from their mistakes but to recognize that the repeated defeats they have suffered might be communicating something.

Mind you, no one in the Magic Resistance or the Democratic Party talked about "gets," or any equivalent of the cascading synchronicities that surrounded the frog god's triumph in 2016. That may be the most significant detail of all the complexities that surrounded the Kek Wars. One of the most pervasive bad habits in pop-culture versions of magic these days is the conviction, as widespread as it is misguided, that all magic—all changes in consciousness in accordance with will—originates with some conscious choice on the part of individual human beings. Traditional occult teaching, by contrast, flatly rejects this claim. The old magical lore is full of ways to figure out which way the winds of magical change are blowing, so that operative mages and human beings generally can trim their sails accordingly and not waste time and effort trying to sail into the teeth of a rising gale.

To the knowledgeable mage, to shift metaphors, human intentions skim this way and that across the surface of very deep waters, while greater shapes follow their own trajectories through the deeps. The question that needs to be asked, in considering the magical dimensions of the Trump phenomenon, is which of the dwellers in the depths is roiling the surface of American politics in our time—and which way it might be headed.

To make sense of those deeper movements of consciousness and politics, a different perspective will be useful. With that in mind, permit me to take you on a virtual journey to a stone tower by the shores of Lake

Zurich in Switzerland, where we'll make the posthumous acquaintance of Carl Jung.

Depending on who you ask, Jung was either a psychologist who knew a lot about occultism or an occultist who managed to fool a great many people into thinking he was talking about psychology. (I tend toward the latter explanation.) Either way, he was one of the twentieth century's most intriguing thinkers, and some of his explorations of the human mind cast a great deal of light on the events we've been discussing.

One of the things he discussed in detail, for example, was exactly the kind of cascade of strange but meaningful coincidences I mentioned in the introduction and discussed in the previous chapter. Jung called these patterns "synchronicities," and argued—in a book he wrote together with Nobel Prize-winning quantum physicist Wolfgang Pauli—that they demonstrate the existence of a web of hidden connections that bind the universe together, in a way that's entirely separate from ordinary cause and effect. In Jung's own clinical practice, he watched synchronicities pile up around patients under certain kinds of serious mental strain, indicating the roots of their problems and pointing the way to healing.

Jung had a lot to say about synchronicity, but the point that's relevant here is that synchroniticies don't show up at random. When you get a flurry of them, especially when they cluster around specific images and ideas, you know that something is moving in the deep reaches of the psyche. What that "something" is, in turn, was the central theme of Jung's researches. He called those moving shapes archetypes. If ordinary thoughts are the little fish that swim near the surface of the mind's sea, archetypes are the great whales that sound the depths. They are clusters of nonrational images knotted together with potent emotional energies, and they provide the human mind with the most basic raw material of thought.

Deep below the surface of the mind, Jung argued, in the crawlspaces of consciousness where the oh-so-rational thinkers of early twentieth century Europe never deigned to look, the same forms and presences that shape ancient myths and magical traditions remained a living presence in every human being. Jung argued that the archetypes are the subjective dimension of human instinct. Newborn goslings look for the nearest large moving object and identify it as Mom, an instinctive mechanism demonstrated amusingly by the famous biologist Konrad Lorenz, who used to get himself adopted as surrogate parent by newly hatched geese. In exactly the same way, if on a somewhat more complex level, infant humans look for a person who corresponds to an inborn mother-image and identify that person as Mom. The inborn mother-image, in Jung's terminology, is the mother archetype.

What makes these images potent in human experience is that they don't go away when their immediate biological usefulness is finished. We all carry around in the deep places of our minds a mother-image, a father-image, a lover-image, an enemy-image, and many others beside these. These images get projected onto actual human beings, in the same way that the Mom-image got projected onto Konrad Lorenz by a flock of goslings—and very often with no better logic. Watch two people fall in love, or talk to somebody who's in the grip of a fanatic hatred of some group of people he's never met, and it's clear that the processes we're talking about have nothing to do with reasoning or any other sort of ordinary thinking.

Much of Jung's work as a psychologist involved listening carefully to the dreams, fantasies, and reflections of his patients, trying to figure out what instinct-images were shaping their thinking and behavior willy-nilly. Thus (to make up an example) he would try to help a patient with an unhealthy mother-fixation to detach the ordinary human being who happened to be his mother from the overwhelming emotional power of the inborn mother-image, so he could replace obsessive emotional patterns with an ordinary relationship between two adult human beings. It was a subtle process, and like most things in human life it wasn't always successful, but it taught Jung to watch carefully when an archetypal image took on a life of its own. That's one thing to keep in mind about archetypes: they aren't passive. They don't just sit there at the bottom of the psyche waiting for someone to notice them.

The easiest way to understand how archetypes work is to follow one of them as it sweeps through the mind. Perhaps the easiest to track is the one Jung called the Shadow. That's the archetype of the enemy, the rival, the hated and feared Other, and what makes it so easy to follow is a detail that psychologists noticed a very long time ago: people consistently assign to the Shadow all the things they absolutely can't bear to face about themselves.

Take a moment to think about a very common human experience that we might as well call "falling in hate." You encounter someone, either in person or via the media, and something about that person rubs you the wrong way. Quickly or slowly, depending on circumstances— some people fall in hate faster than others—that person stands out from among all the ordinarily annoying people you know. Every word from his mouth and every expression on his features grate on your nerves; he radiates hatefulness from every pore; you can't see his face without thinking about how much it needs to be punched. No matter how hard you try, you can't be objective where the object of your hate is concerned, and if the process goes far enough, you stop being able to have conversations with people who don't share your views—for some reason they keep on acting as though your reasonable criticism of the object of your dislike is saliva-flecked ranting full of seething hatred.

From Jung's perspective, what's happened here is that the archetype of the Shadow has seized your thinking and projected itself through you onto another person. While that projection is in force, you literally can't think clearly about the other person, because every thought you have concerning him or her is swept up in the movement of the archetype. It's as though rage-colored goggles suddenly drop over your eyes the moment you look at the target of the projection. The secret of that rage, in turn, is that everything you say about the target of your projections is something you can't stand about yourself. If you scream "Liar!" at him, anyone who knows how projection works will realize that you're acutely uncomfortable about your own dishonesty; if you shriek "Bully!" at him, your own bullying propensities are on display, and so on.

It's worth noting here that the things that get projected onto the Shadow needn't be bad in any conventional sense. In an earlier chapter I mentioned the Traditionalist thinker Julius Evola. Read his writings and you'll find them full of contempt toward the modern world for its softness and its humanitarianism—this latter is a dirty word in Evola's vocabulary. What was going on, to judge from accounts written by people who knew Evola in person, was that he loathed his own capacities for kindness, gentleness, and compassion, and so loaded them onto the Shadow he projected onto the society around him. The *Revolt Against the Modern World* he wrote about in his most famous book, as such things always are, was ultimately a revolt against himself.

How do you tell the difference between ordinary reasonable hatred and the projection of the Shadow? It's quite simple, though "simple" is not the same thing as "easy." Archetypes are absolute, while human beings never are. In the worst human being there are still admirable features, just as there are despicable features in the best of our species. If you can look at the object of your hatred and, with a little thought, list a number of things about that person you find admirable—not ironically or sarcastically, but honestly admirable—you're probably not caught up in the Shadow archetype. If you can't do this, you're probably projecting the Shadow, and if you get furious at the very thought that anyone would suggest that there's even the smallest thing admirable about the person you hate . . . well, you can fill in the blank here as well as I can.

The Shadow is just one of the archetypes. There are many others. When you fall head over heels in love, for example, what's happened is that a different archetype—Jung calls it the Anima or Animus, depending on gender and sexual orientation—has been projected onto the other person, with effects that have the same potency but the opposite emotional charge as in a Shadow projection. All of the most intense human interactions are mediated by one or more archetypes. Yet not all archetypes apply to all people; there are universal human archetypes, and then there are archetypes that are specific to smaller subsets of humanity.

Jung wrote about one of these with unnerving prescience in his harrowing 1936 essay "Wotan." At a time when most people in Europe believed that the funny little man with the Charlie Chaplin mustache who'd become Chancellor of Germany was a third-rate Mussolini wannabe who would be out of office as soon as German politics went through another of its routine convulsions, Jung grasped that something far deeper and more terrifying was in motion. What was happening in Germany, he argued, couldn't be understood so long as it was forced into the mental straitjacket of politics as usual. The paired languages of myth on the one hand, and psychopathology on the other, alone made adequate sense of what amounted to an impending psychotic break that would affect not individuals but continents. "A hurricane has broken loose in Germany," he wrote, "while we still believe it is fine weather."

That hurricane, Jung suggested, was the activation of an archetype that belonged not to all of humanity but specifically to the people who live in central Europe, where the immense sweep of the Eurasian plains to the east breaks against the rumpled hills and river valleys that run between the Alps and the North Sea. That archetype was associated with the myths of the archaic god Wotan. These days, most people who remember the deity in question think of his near-equivalent Odin, whose deeds and impending doom are celebrated in Old Norse poetry, or of the literary creation who plays a central role in Richard Wagner's *Ring of the Nibelung* operas, but there is also a distinctive version of Wotan in German folklore, a terrifying huntsman-figure who rides the storm winds, leading a vast army of ghosts through the midnight skies.

Whether gods are the reflections of archetypes or archetypes are the reflections of gods is a moot point for the present purpose. The point that's relevant here is that Jung caught something that nearly everyone else in his time missed. For decades, since the twilight years of the nineteenth century, something had been stirring in the German-speaking lands of central Europe, something that shook off the heavy-handed rationalism of a confident age and plunged into the deep places where human consciousness merged with the forces of nature. In the wake of a lost war and a bitter economic depression, that archetypal force seized on an unlikely vehicle—an Austrian artist and bohemian turned political agitator named Adolf Hitler—and swept up most of Europe into a maelstrom that ended, as the myths of Wotan always end, in Götterdammerung.

The cascade of synchronicities that surrounded Donald Trump's 2016 campaign suggests to me that something not dissimilar is at work in today's America. Wotan is not an American archetype, however. While the Wild Hunt has its American equivalent—fans of old-fashioned country music will recall the classic piece "Ghost Riders in the Sky"—the Lord of the Slain on his eight-legged horse Sleipnir is absent in that song, and in American myth and folklore generally. We must look elsewhere for the archetype at work in today's politics.

The brilliant Native American philosopher and activist Vine Deloria Jr. offered a vital hint in his most influential work, *God Is Red*. He pointed out that in the wake of the Reformation, Western spirituality lost track of a crucial variable—the spiritual importance of place. To most spiritual traditions, and to Native American traditions even more than most, specific places on the land have their own unique spiritual properties and powers, which are not dependent on the people who happen to live there. He went on to argue that much of the reason why modern American society stumbles so blindly from one preventable disaster to another is that we have not yet learned to relate in a sacred manner to the powers of place, the spirits of the land on which we live—and that those powers remain the ones that native peoples reverenced. Thus it seems to me that there's a specific mythic figure whose archetype is in play just now.

A great many native myths, from across the length and breadth of North America, tell of a being whose task it is to change the world so that the people can live there. Among the Salish-speaking tribes of southern Puget Sound, for example, the Changer is Moon; among the Takelma, who live in far southwestern Oregon, he's Daldal the dragon-fly; in some parts of the dryland West he's Coyote, and so on. In some stories he's a hero, in some he's a buffoon, in some he's an incomprehensible force of nature. The details vary, but the basic theme remains the same. The world was different once, say the tales, and then the Changer came and made it the way it is now.

The versions of the Changer story I know best have a distinctive episodic shape. In one Puget Sound version, for example, after a long and intricate backstory, Moon leaves the land of the salmon people under the sea and starts walking up the Snoqualmie River toward the mountains. All the beings who live in that country know that he's coming, and they prepare weapons and traps to stop him, because they don't want him to change the world and make it ready for the people when they come. So he meets a man who's sitting at the water's edge carving a board out of wood. "What are you doing?" Moon asks him, and the man says, "There's someone coming who's going to change things, and I'm going to hit him over the head with this board and kill him." Moon takes the board, sticks it onto the man's rump, and says, "From now on your name is Beaver. When the people come they'll hunt you for your fur."

Moon goes further up the river, and he sees another man who's looking anxiously around from the top of a hill. He has two weapons, one in each hand, and they have many sharp points. "What are you doing?" Moon asks him, and the man says, "There's someone coming who's going to change things, and I'm going to stab him with all these points and kill him." Moon takes the weapons, sticks them on the man's head, and says, "From now on your name is Deer. When the people come they'll hunt you for your meat and your hide."

And so the story goes. In the hands of a skilled storyteller—and storytelling is one of the fine arts in Native American cultures—the story of the Changer can be spun out to any length desired, with any number of lively incidents meant to point up morals or pass on nuggets of wisdom. There's no rising spiral of action leading to a grand battle between the Changer and the beings whose world he has come to change. There's just one incident after another, until the Changer finally reaches the source of the Snoqualmie River and leaps into the sky to become the Moon, leaving the world forever different in his wake.

Notice just how often this pattern is repeated in American history, in the great changes that transform our public life for good or ill. Almost never do you see a single great struggle in which everything is decided. Where the battle of Waterloo came at the end of the Napoleonic Wars and settled them once and for all, our nearest equivalent, Gettysburg, came only a little more than midway through the Civil War, and simply marked the high tide of the Confederacy, the point from which all roads finally led to Appomattox. The changes that matter very often focus around one person who becomes the focus of change, and who proceeds up the river of our national life, encountering one crisis after another and somehow overcoming each one of them, until death or retirement ends the tale—and by the time that happens, the world has changed decisively and nothing will ever be the same again.

That's the archetypal pattern unfolding in American life right now. I don't know of a Native American myth in which the Changer's role is played by a frog with magic powers, or for that matter by a King in Orange, but those images do seem to describe the situation we're in.

Two features of the Changer myth seem particularly relevant at the moment. The first is pointed up skillfully in the stories. The beings who try to stop the Changer keep doing whatever they were doing when the Changer arrives: the man with the board keeps carving tree trunks, the man with the many-pointed weapons keeps looking around—and there they are today, the beaver by his dam, the deer on the hill. Having refused change, they became unable to change, and went through the motions of their failed plans forever. That's exactly what Trump's opponents have been doing since his candidacy hit its stride in 2015. ("From now on your name is Protester," says the Changer, and sticks a pussy hat on the woman's head and a placard in her hands. "When the people come they'll meme you for the keks.")

The flipside of the same narrative can be traced in Trump's own trajectory. Ever since the beginning of his campaign, his opponents have convinced themselves that this or that or the other thing will surely stop him. They tried to hit him over the head with an investigation and stab him with an impeachment, but incident followed incident, and he just kept going up the river and changing things. There's never the grand dénouement they wanted so desperately; even the 2020 election turned into a cascade of incidents, not the decisive event they hoped for. The crisis never comes—and what's more, it never will come.

That's one of the things about archetypes. When one of them finds a human vehicle and begins to reshape the collective life of a society in its image, if you know the archetype you can know in advance how things will unfold. Jung didn't make many predictions in the essay of his I cited earlier, but it should have been obvious from the start that once the Wotan-archetype found its vehicle and seized the German imagination, it would make a beeline for Ragnarok. What's more, after his death, Hitler continued to fulfill the myth, becoming the modern world's Lord of the Slain, galloping forever through the midnight skies of our collective imagination with six million wailing ghosts following in his wake.

Wotan is not the Changer, and different archetypes pursue different destinies. To understand where the Changer is headed and what destiny awaits the world after his passing, it's going to be necessary to take an even deeper plunge, into the first stirrings of a future that few if any of our society's talking heads have begun to grasp.

6

The Hands of the Living God

Magical Cultures Past, Present, and to Come

And now I heard his voice, rising, swelling, thundering through the flaring light, and as I fell, the radiance increasing, increasing, poured over me in waves of flame. Then I sank into the depths, and I heard the King in Yellow whispering in my soul: "It is a fearful thing to fall into the hands of the living God!"

FROM "IN THE COURT OF THE DRAGON"
IN *THE KING IN YELLOW*

If you pay close attention to your own dreams and fantasies, you can learn to see archetypes stirring into motion long before they project themselves on the people around you. If you pay close attention to the dreams and fantasies of a nation, the same principle applies. That's what Jung did in "Wotan." He noticed that a particular set of archetypal images linked with the old German god Wotan—the Wild Huntsman, the god of magic, madness, and death—had stirred to new life in the German psyche, with consequences that Jung guessed at dimly, and the rest of Europe learned about in a much less pleasant way shortly thereafter.

Watch the dreams and fantasies of a nation, in other words, and you can catch the foreshadowing of its future—sometimes. There's another side to the autonomy of the archetypes, though. Just as they don't wait passively for us to act upon them, they also don't show up on cue. Jung could write what he did, when he did, because the storm was about to break and it took merely a keen eye to catch the flickering of the lightning on the horizon. Friedrich Nietzsche, half a century before him, recognized that Europe would plunge into a nightmare vortex of ideological warfare once the twentieth century dawned, but he misjudged completely what the ruling ideologies would be. Heinrich Heine, another half century further back, could only catch a dim sense that the gods of Germanic antiquity were stirring and that war would follow them.

The cultural history of nineteenth- and early twentieth-century Central Europe maps out, with remarkable clarity, the process by which one archetype loses its grip on a society and another rises with glacial slowness to replace it. The archetype that was fading out in those years was embodied in the old Ghibelline ideal of the Holy Roman Empire— aristocratic, Christian, shaped by the legacies of classical culture, centered on a vision of human community that balanced intense local loyalties with a commitment to an imperial institution that transcended nations, creeds, and languages.

One of the most striking symptoms of that ideal's twilight was the number of voices raised in increasingly shrill tones to insist that it was still thriving. The Austro-Hungarian Empire claimed, with no shortage of historical precedent, to embody that ideal. After 1871, when the German Empire was founded, its propagandists did their level best to hijack the ideal's prestige. After crisis hit in 1914, the former quietly imploded, while the latter metastasized into something that had no connection with the Ghibelline ideal at all—so drastic was the difference that the German aristocracy, which clung to the old vision with a fierceness that was only sharpened by its futility, became the spawning ground for the most effective resistance movements Hitler's regime faced.

Yet the old ideal was as dead as the proverbial doornail long before the First World War pushed it into an unmarked grave. The cause of death was the same thing that normally dooms such ideals, the immense gap that had opened up over time between the archetype and the increasingly sordid and pedestrian realities on which it was projected. In a certain ironic sense, history was doing for central Europe what Carl Jung did for his patients—drawing a distinction between the emotionally powerful image and the underwhelming reality—but of course there was a catch, for the departure of one archetype doesn't mean the end of the projection mechanism, nor does it guarantee that the one that rises in its place will be an improvement.

Such reflections are embarrassingly rare these days. It's all but unheard of for anyone in American public life to stop and say aloud, "Hold it. Is the place toward which we're progressing someplace that any sane person would want to go?" Of course one of the reasons so few people do this is that those who do get shouted down as impractical dreamers, and the mere fact that the so-called dreamers are so often right, and the practical men of affairs who dismiss them are so often wrong, somehow never inspires the least willingness to rethink the matter.

This is where Oswald Spengler, whose work on the cycles of history has been mentioned already in this study, comes into his own. His major work *The Decline of the West* has yielded one accurate prediction after another while the futures predicted by his critics, by turns utopian and apocalyptic, have all proved as evanescent as moonbeams. Drawing on earlier scholars such as Giambattista Vico, Spengler set out a theory of the morphology of civilizations, tracing them through the stages of a life cycle—birth, youth, maturity, senility, and death—that guided his predictions about the future of Western or, as he called it, Faustian culture.

Central to Spengler's theory, and just as central to the spluttering denunciations leveled at him by the defenders of the conventional wisdom ever since his time, is the recognition that "progress" is a mythological concept rather than a historical reality. Classical civilization—Apollonian culture, in his terminology—was not a step forward past the mark left by ancient Egypt. Equally, what Spengler called the Magian culture, the high culture in the Middle East that culminated with the Islamic Caliphate in what we call the Middle Ages, was not a step past Apollonian culture, and our Faustian culture is no more advanced than any of those I've named.

Does that sound like a paradox? It's nothing of the kind. Each great culture has its own values and goals and priorities, which it fulfills as well as circumstances permit. Our Faustian culture seems more "progressive" to us for no better reason than because it's gone further in the direction of fulfilling the values and goals and priorities of Faustian culture than anyone else. Apollonian culture invented the steam engine and the gear train, the two great technological breakthroughs that launched Faustian culture on its way to temporary global dominion, but the Greek and Roman engineers who dabbled in such things didn't value the things that Gerbert of Aurillac and James Watt did, and so didn't put them to the same uses. Most other great cultures weren't interested enough in such things even to dabble.

Thus it's an embarrassing bit of ethnocentrism to insist, as so many writers of alternate-history novels have done, that if Western Europeans hadn't gotten around to inventing steam engines, gear trains, and the rest of the toolkit that made the industrial world happen, someone else would have. Our technology is a Faustian technology, shaped throughout by the passions and obsessive ideas of the great culture that was born in western and central Europe around the year 1000. As Faustian culture winds down—a process already well under way—its technology can be expected to settle into a static mold, shed those elements that aren't sustainable, and be mined as a resource by future great cultures, the way Greek logic and mathematics were mined by the Indian, Magian, and Faustian cultures for purposes entirely their own.

Let's take a look off into the future with that in mind, and try to get a sense of what's likely to happen as Faustian culture finishes settling down into its final stasis. One point that Spengler makes is particularly important in this context. However far afield a great culture may extend its power during its period of imperial expansion, it remains rooted in its original homelands, and once the inevitable age of empire suffers its equally inevitable decline and fall, its far-flung extensions fall away and the original homelands of the culture hold onto what's left of it until some later culture brushes it aside.

Faustian culture, as already noted, had its origins in western and central Europe. In its time of empire, between 1492 and 1914, it surged out of Europe to conquer and pillage most of the planet. Though its prestige is still high enough that privileged classes over most of the world still wear clothes of European style and maintain governments of European type, it's very much a waning power at this point. Our task is to glimpse, through the lens of our current political convulsions, what comes after.

As a great culture goes into decline, the places to watch are the borderlands. These aren't necessarily the political borders, though they can be. As Apollonian culture slid down the well-greased chute of decline and fall, for example, two border regions turned out to be of crucial importance. One was the eastern border zone where the Mediterranean littoral blended with deserts and then with the ancient cities of Persia and the Arabian peninsula, where Rome's military power never reached but its cultural and economic influence was strong. The other centered on the valleys of half a dozen large rivers that flowed into the North Sea, among them the Thames, the Seine, and the Rhine, where Roman power established itself for a while and then lost its grip as the age of migrations began.

Both of those areas proceeded to birth great cultures of their own. In the east, what Spengler called the Magian culture began to take shape long before Rome fell, and succeeded in absorbing the Byzantine empire into its own ambit once the western empire was gone. In the West, where the collapse of Rome had much more drastic impacts, a long and difficult dark age passed before Faustian culture began to emerge. In each case, though, the emerging culture started out borrowing a set of existing forms inherited from an older great culture.

Spengler calls this process "pseudomorphosis." You can see it with impressive clarity in the history of Western architecture, among many

other places. The standard building style in early medieval Europe
is called Romanesque nowadays, and for very good reason: it looks
like a halfhearted copy of Roman architecture. A few centuries went
by, and then the pseudomorphosis was shaken off and Gothic architecture soared skyward, at the same time as the first great flowering
of Faustian cultural forms in other arts and sciences broke free of
Apollonian models.

Magian culture had its comparable era of pseudomorphosis earlier,
and from a different source. (Spengler didn't see this, but he was working with a far less complete understanding of Middle Eastern archeology
than we have now.) Magian culture originally began to draw together in
the aftermath of the Mesopotamian culture, and in its early days it borrowed many of the forms and habits of the great cultural tradition that
had its origins in the mud-brick towns of Sumer. When Apollonian culture expanded into the Magian heartlands—first under Alexander the
Great, then under an assortment of Greek-speaking empires, and finally
under the eagles of Rome—there followed a second era of pseudomorphosis, followed by a sharp reaction against the Apollonian influence.
Rabbinic Judaism, eastern Christianity, Islam, and a flurry of less successful faiths such as Manichaeanism surged outward in response, cast
aside Apollonian political, cultural, and creative forms, and established
the Magian world on their ruins.

And Faustian culture? It also had two eras of pseudomorphosis.
The first, as already noted, drew on the heritage of Rome. The second,
later on, drew on Magian culture. From the Middle Ages to the early
modern period, it's no exaggeration—though it's a blow to European
vanity, no doubt—to see the quarrelling little countries of Europe as
simply a northwestern extension of the vast and prosperous Magian cultural sphere, which extended at its peak from Morocco to Indonesia.

Like the other societies within the Magian sphere, after all, the
nations of Europe were ruled by hereditary monarchs who claimed to
rule as the servants of the one true God. These nations had established
dogmatic religions from which dissent was permitted only in strictly

limited ways, guided by a sacred scripture, centered in a holy city, and expressed in formal congregational worship on a specific day of the week, which everyone was expected to attend. These and a galaxy of other Magian customs were standard across Europe—it's not accidental that European Traditionalists so reliably turn back to the Middle East for inspiration, since not only the traditions they follow but the entire notion of one true unchanging Tradition handed down from the beginning of time, and only accessible to those who belong to an established religious body, is a Magian invention.

Yet that turned out to be a passing phase, just as the Apollonian pseudomorphosis turned out to be a passing phase for the Magian culture some centuries further back. As Faustian culture began to waken to its own possibilities, Magian forms were cast aside or twisted completely out of their original shapes. European master builders who learned Arabic architectural innovations reshaped them, producing the soaring vertical lines and pointed arches of the Gothic era; monks tinkering with the old Apollonian technology of gear trains reworked it to allow the transmission of power, creating not only the mechanical clock but an essential part of most of the mechanical technologies that followed from it; Aristotelian physics got reworked to permit the introduction of concepts of impetus and force that were completely foreign to Apollonian natural science, but essential to the rise of Faustian science.

All this was effectively unimaginable from the point of view of Apollonian culture. Imagine, for a moment, the predicament of a perceptive thinker in late Apollonian society—say, a Greek philosopher living around 250 CE—who had grasped the reality of his society's decline and guessed at the broader pattern of historical cycles in which that decline played one of the standard parts. Our philosopher might just possibly guess that the next great culture in the part of the world he knew about might rise out of the eastern penumbra of Roman civilization. His chances of getting any kind of advance notion of the shape of the rising Magian culture, though, were miniscule. To focus on only one detail, how easily could a person raised to think of religion as a matter of traditional rites about which you could believe anything you wanted, so long as you performed them, imagine a religion where belief in a particular set of opinions was so important that people slaughtered one another over minute differences of creed?

For that matter, the chance that our philosopher could have anticipated the rise of another great culture out of the northwestern borderlands of the Roman world was probably too small to worry about. In 250 CE, the valleys of the Thames, the Seine, and the Rhine were about as central to the Roman world as the valleys of the Missouri, the Ohio, and the Tennessee Rivers are to the modern European world, and the thought that a great culture could emerge from what was then a cultural backwater inhabited by barbarian deplorables would have seemed utterly absurd if anyone had gotten around to thinking of it at all.

We're in a similar situation today, of course. The great culture that is settling into its static form, and will play a greatly diminished role in the history of the world from now on, is Faustian culture—the great culture that rose in those northwestern borderlands of Rome in the wake of the Dark Ages, contended with Magian culture as that latter passed its own zenith and settled into the normal static condition, and then surged out across the globe to conquer most of the planet's land surface and impose its idiosyncratic cultural fashions on nearly every society on Earth.

Like the Apollonian culture, Faustian culture also has two major borderlands, one to the east of its heartlands, one to the west, and from those we can probably expect the rise of two more great cultures in due time. There may be others as well; West Africa and certain regions of Latin America strike me as very likely to birth high cultures in the millennium ahead; but for the moment, for reasons that will become clear as we proceed, I want to talk about the two border regions already mentioned. Those borderlands? Today we call them Russia and America: specifically, European Russia west of the Urals, especially the region centering on the Volga valley, and North America west of the

Appalachians, especially the region centering on the Ohio and upper Mississippi valleys and the Great Lakes littoral.

The parallels with the Apollonian experience go surprisingly deep, because something like the same difference in age that shaped the relative histories of the Magian and Faustian cultures seems likely to shape the equivalent trajectories of the Russian and American cultures to come. Russia passed through its first pseudomorphosis a good many centuries back in its early formative period, when it absorbed potent cultural influences from the Byzantine Empire, at that time an important part of the Magian cultural sphere. It began its second pseudomorphosis in the days of Peter the Great, when a new set of cultural influences from the Faustian culture to the west swept over Russia. It's currently early on in the inevitable reaction, which will see both the Byzantine and the European influences give way to the first bold statements of a distinctively Russian high culture. This is something that occultists have been talking about for a long time, by the way, and the consensus is that this process will begin late in the present century.

North America, by contrast, received what Magian influence it had at second hand, by way of Magian elements retained by Faustian culture, and its first pseudomorphosis began in the early seventeenth century when the first waves of European settlement surged across a landscape mostly depopulated by the cataclysmic impact of Old World diseases on the native peoples. The second pseudomorphosis hasn't happened yet, and it's an interesting question which of the great cultures of the next millennium will be responsible for that challenging stimulus. One way or another, it'll be after the second pseudomorphosis sparks its inevitable reaction that the first bold statements of a distinctively American high culture will appear. Here again, occultists have been discussing this dimension of our future for quite some time now, and the consensus is that this will probably get under way sometime in the twenty-sixth century.

Meanwhile both the nascent great cultures of the borderlands have a Faustian pseudomorphosis to deal with. In today's America, in particular, it's a massive issue. To make sense of it, it's important to grasp the way that pseudomorphosis depends on the activities of an intelligentsia. That's a Russian word originally, but it came into being—as plenty of words in many languages come into being—by taking a word from one language and slapping onto it a grammatical suffix from a different language. This is roughly the process by which an intelligentsia comes into being, too. The intelligentsia comprises those people who belong to one culture but who are educated in the ideas, customs, and practices of another.

That can happen because the first culture is conquered by the second, and the new overlords proceed to impose their own cultural forms on their new domain. It can also happen because the elite classes of the first culture, in order to compete in a world dominated by the second culture, adopt the second culture's ideas and habits as far as they can. For an example of the first category, think of the native schoolteachers and minor bureaucrats recruited by European colonial empires all through the nineteenth century. For an example of the second, think of those African and Asian nations today that have parliaments, build skyscrapers in their capitals, and outfit their elite classes in business suits and neckties.

Members of the intelligentsia are the foot soldiers of pseudomorphosis. They're the ones whose task it is to take the foreign cultural forms they have embraced and impose them, by persuasion or force, on other members of their society. There are inevitably sharp limits to how far they can take this process; pushback is guaranteed, and since the intelligentsia is always a small minority the pushback can't just be brushed aside. That's where you get the standard pattern of a colonial society, with a cosmopolitan elite class (either foreign or native), a native intelligentsia aspiring to a cosmopolitan status its members will never attain, and the vast and sullen laboring classes that regard with smoldering hostility the intelligentsia and the foreign culture it promotes.

The position of the intelligentsia, privileged as it is, thus has its bitter downsides. On the one hand, they are hated and despised by the members of the vast and sullen laboring classes just mentioned. On the other, they can never quite win the approval of the foreign elites whose ways they so sedulously imitate. Neither fish nor fowl nor good red meat, the intelligentsia are caught in the gap between cultures, and within the limits of the worldview that emerges in a colonial society, there's no way out of their predicament. They never succeed either in converting the masses to the ways of the foreign culture they've embraced, on the one hand, or in being fully accepted by the people who belong to that foreign culture on the other.

What breaks the intelligentsia out of its predicament, rather, are precisely those things that its members fear most. To begin with, there's personal failure. The overproduction of educated managerial personnel discussed earlier is a constant feature of such societies, so the numbers of the intelligentsia always balloon past what the job market for schoolteachers, minor bureaucrats, and other similar positions can take in. The result is an explosive far more dangerous than mere dynamite: an educated underclass that has been cast aside by the system, after its members have been taught to understand their position and given the skills with which they can organize opposition to the existing order of things.

Then there's the second factor, which is that no dominant culture retains its dominance forever. One way or another, the high tide of political power and cultural charisma is always followed by the running of the waters back out to sea. As the dominant culture loses its ascendancy, the intelligentsia no longer has a ready market for its only stock in trade, and the pushback from the laboring classes gains in strength.

The first thing that happens then is that the educated underclass, composed of people who have been trained for the intelligentsia but failed to claw their way into the jobs for which they have been prepared, makes common cause with the laboring classes. The twilight years of Europe's Third World colonies have plenty of examples of that first dynamic. What pushes things over the edge into rapid change is that members of the intelligentsia who aren't part of the underclass, who got the good jobs and the prestigious positions under the colonial regime, notice what's happening, weigh their options, and side with the underclass and the masses. You've probably heard of a man named Gandhi.

Read the first half or so of any good biography of him and you'll see that second dynamic written in letters ten feet tall.

All this is essential to understanding our current situation. North America and Russia are still, culturally speaking, European colonies. The elite classes in both nations ape the fashions and habits of wealthy Europeans just as sedulously as do the elite classes of so many Third World nations. The architecture of both nation's major cities, the art forms that the urban elites consume so avidly, even the clothing styles on display, are all European inventions. That's par for the course in cultural colonies or, to put the same thing in Spengler's terms, in societies under the influence of pseudomorphosis from a dominant culture.

It doesn't actually make that much of a difference that political power slipped out of the hands of European elites most of a century ago, and they and their nations play second fiddle to the rulers of the really important borderland nations. The same thing happened more than two millennia ago when Greece fell under Roman domination. Roman patricians still paraded their knowledge of Greek culture and decorated their villas with statues bought in Greece the way American millionaires used to snap up European paintings to decorate mansions and museums in Los Angeles and Omaha. The cultural charisma of the older society remains in place, at the level of the privileged elite and the intelligentsia that members of the elite hire and fire at will.

As I've never lived in Russia, and my exposure to Russian culture has mostly been through reading literature written by dead people, I can't state from personal experience how precisely the colonial structure of society fits what's going on there. Here in America, on the other hand, I've got the advantage of lifelong residence spent in a variety of regions, and the match is exact. We've got our cosmopolitan elite class, wallowing in the absurd displays of extravagance common to any empire in its diminuendo phase. We've got our intelligentsia, caught in the usual bind, fretting at their exclusion from the classes above them, and unable to convince the classes below them to adopt the European ideas and habits that are their only stock in trade. We've got our educated failures, who are learning how to take their knowledge of European ideas and find ways to apply it against the interests of the intelligentsia and their masters—yes, that's where I fit into the picture, along with millions of others. Finally, we've got the vast and sullen laboring classes who regard the intelligentsia and their ideas with hatred and contempt, and whose pushback against the pseudomorphosis being thrust on them has become a political fact of immense importance. Spell those labels "investment class," "salary class," "basement brigade," and "wage class," and you have exactly the divergences we've been exploring all through this book.

The American intelligentsia, it is worth noting, has been caught up in a specifically European pseudomorphosis for as long as there's been an American intelligentsia. The focus of their dreams has shifted over the course of its history, to be sure. From colonial days to the beginning of the twentieth century, members of the intelligentsia here in the United States aped the English; during the first two-thirds or so of the twentieth century, France was the usual focus of such obsessions—I'm thinking here among many other things of the wry offhand comment by British author Somerset Maugham, in his novel *The Razor's Edge,* that France was where good Americans hoped to go when they died.

These days it's usually the Scandinavian countries that provide the model on which members of the American intelligentsia consciously or half-consciously model their dreams of what they want the United States to become. (It's a habit that my Scandinavian friends find baffling, for whatever that's worth.) A few years ago a book, *The Almost Nearly Perfect People: Behind the Myth of the Scandinavian Utopia* by Michael Booth, tried to disabuse readers in the English-speaking world of their habit of idolizing the Nordic countries. As far as I can tell, it didn't accomplish much, and if it had, the people at whom it was aimed would simply have found some other European country to hold up as an ideal. In America, it's essential to the self-concept of the intelligentsia to pretend not to be American, and to make a show of contempt for their own cultural and ethnic backgrounds. That's how they prove to themselves that they don't belong to "*those* people," the ordinary deplorable Americans the intelligentsia love to despise.

The difficulties faced by the American intelligentsia in their hopeless quest to Europeanize the United States, however, go beyond the usual factors that make such projects exercises in futility. Crucially, at the ideological core of European civilization lies the conviction that all human history is a prelude to Europe; that what Europe is now, all other societies will inevitably become; that Europe is uniquely modern, and any society that isn't copying Europe down to the fine details needs to catch up to the cutting edge of the future, which is (again) Europe. No doubt that's very comforting to believe, but it doesn't happen to be true.

The pervasive confusion that equates "European" to "modern," and consigns everything else to a notional past, is an immense barrier to understanding just now. Europe is what it is, and has the habits it has, because of the convoluted legacies of a couple of millennia of extremely idiosyncratic history. Wherever that history didn't happen, the forms of European culture are a shallow veneer over a very different substrate, and show no signs of taking deeper root. It's essential to the worldview and the self-concept of the American intelligentsia that this should not be the case, since their worlds revolve around the conviction that someday Arkansas will have the attitudes and cultural habits that Boston has today—by which time, of course, Boston will presumably be indistinguishable from a European city, or more precisely from the fantasy of what a European city ought to be that haunts the American intelligentsia's collective imagination.

Now of course the cities of Europe, even those in Scandinavia, don't have much in common with the fantasy just indicated. Europe is going through its own hard transition right now, driven by conflicts of a sort we also have over here—the inevitable struggle, discussed at some length by Spengler, between elitist plutocracy disguised as democracy on the one hand, and populist Caesarism backed by the masses on the other. (May I risk a spoiler? In the long run, this isn't a struggle the plutocrats can win.)

There's another factor at work, however, and it's the one that we discussed earlier: the pervasive link, hard to define but perilous to ignore, that binds a civilization to the broad region in which it arose. In the United States, it's not hard to catch the difference between those regions that were part of the preindustrial European world—the old coastal settlements of the Atlantic seaboard—and the vast hinterlands left untouched until after Europe had finished its cultural development (in Spengler's view, this happened around 1800). I live across the Seekonk River from Providence, Rhode Island. There, as the Eagles sang back in the day, "the old world's shadows hang heavy in the air." Walk the streets of Providence today and you'll taste something distinctly half-European in the ambience there. You can find the same thing in other colonial towns such as Lancaster, Pennsylvania, which were spared the ravages of twentieth-century urban renewal, and even in some towns that suffered from that blight.

Go west into the Appalachians or beyond them and that vanishes utterly. What replaces it is a sense of something still raw and unformed, moving in the dark silent soil under the strip malls and subdivisions, reaching clumsily as yet toward some fulfillment whose shape has not yet become clear. That's something that writers and poets have been sensing in the American land for a couple of centuries now. Back in the days of frontier expansion, that sense got taken (in my view, mistaken) for an awareness of the potential of the European-American settlement. Later, in the heyday of U.S. empire, it got tangled up in a collective daydream that saw an Anglo-American imperium as the Universal State that would bring peace to a Europeanized world.

The frontier closed well over a century ago, and the temporary hegemony of the United States over most of the world is cracking around us as I write this, but I've felt the same sense of something stirring as I've walked various corners of the American land. It reminds me of the "Buffalo Wind" that Canadian naturalist and author Ernest Thompson

Seton wrote about so movingly in his essays, the sense of a land preg-nant with the future that American poet Robinson Jeffers explored just as powerfully in his verse. I've never had the chance to walk along the Volga and see if something parallel stirs in the earth and the wind, offering a foretaste of another great culture on its way to manifestation. Even so, I'd be willing to bet that it's there.

The political convulsions we're witnessing right now in the United States, I suggest, are best understood as part of the process by which the European pseudomorphosis will be shaken off over the next century or two. That a large part of our intelligentsia is appalled by this comes as no surprise. They're going to have many more opportunities for shriek-ing in the years ahead, and some opportunities for celebration as well. The process we're discussing isn't something that will be accomplished in a few years, or even in a lifespan. To judge by the evidence of history, it will play out in the usual fashion, in something fairly close to the usual time frame.

That way of thinking about history is foreign to most of us these days, and there are reasons for that. Every great culture, to use Spengler's phrase, has its own vision of what the future ought to be like. In Apollonian culture, for example, the future everyone expected was the present endlessly prolonged. The vision of time and change that guided Apollonian culture in the centuries of its maturity had three phases: first, things were in chaos, then a mighty power arose to set things in order, and finally that order endured forever. In religious terms, the mighty power was the god Jupiter taming the Titans with his thunderbolts; in political terms, the mighty power was the Roman Empire bringing the warring kingdoms of the world under its sway; the same logic applied to classical philosophy, which sought to teach the rational mind how to reduce the chaos of the self into an enduring order, and so on.

In Magian culture, that vision found few takers once the Apollonian pseudomorphosis faded out. The Magian vision of time and change, rather, is the one familiar to most of us through its fading reflections in Christian theology. The universe in the Magian view is a stage on which the mighty drama of human salvation is played out. It runs in a straight line from Creation, through the revelation of the one true faith, to a cataclysmic finale, after which nothing will ever change again. At the center of the Magian experience, in turn, is the sense of being part of the community of the faithful, resisting the powers of evil while waiting prayerfully for the one true God to bring on the apocalypse.

Faustian culture still carries remnants of Magian culture with it, which were picked up through the normal process of pseudomorphosis and remain more or less fossilized. At the heart of the Faustian worldview, though, stands a vision of time and change starkly opposed to the Magian vision, and reminiscent of the Apollonian vision only in a highly qualified sense.

In the Faustian vision, it's not chaos that characterizes the original shape of things, it's stasis. Think of all those old childrens' stories about the first caveman to discover fire, or the echo of the same mythic narrative in the opening scenes of Stanley Kubrick's movie *2001: A Space Odyssey,* or the richly embroidered folk mythology that surrounds the Scientific Revolution. For that matter, think of the rhetoric that still frames every one of the grand crusades for social betterment that hasn't yet crumpled under the weight of its failure and turned to Magian apocalypticism instead. (When a social movement in the modern Western world retreats to the Magian pseudomorphosis and starts shouting "The world will end if we don't get what we want!" you can safely bet that it's already failed, and its days are numbered.)

The Faustian story starts in darkness and squalor and stasis, with everyone trudging through age-old routines under the leaden weight of superstition and ignorance. Then some bright individual has the "Aha!" moment that changes everything. He—it's usually a man, at least in the myths—then has to do battle with the forces of superstition and ignorance, but of course he wins in the end. Darkness and squalor give way to something shiny and new, stasis gives way to motion, everyone joyously abandons superstition and ignorance, and the grand march of progress takes another great forward step toward the stars.

That's where the Faustian myth seems to depart furthest from its Apollonian equivalent, but the difference is less important than it looks. The word *progress,* after all, literally means "continued movement in the same direction." In the Faustian myth, the pace of progress can change but the direction can't. That's why, to cite an example, the scientific establishment engaged in an orgy of pearl-clutching in the 1970s when circles of avant-garde researchers started to find common ground with mystics and occultists. The definition of progress accepted then and now in the scientific mainstream consigned mystics and occultists to the dustbin of superstition and ignorance, and the so-called skeptic movement was the inevitable backlash.

It's easy to make fun of the dogmatism and intolerance of the insufficiently skeptical skeptics who believed devoutly that they were fighting against dogmatism and intolerance, but their unholy holy war was a necessary consequence of the central logic of the Faustian cult of progress. Since, by definition, progress is what brought us here out of the squalor and ignorance of the benighted past, and since, by definition, continued movement in the same direction is going to lead us onward and upward to a shining techno-utopian future, any attempt to question the scientific community's rejection of spiritual experiences can only be seen as a surrender to the forces of superstition and ignorance that alone can deny us all our destiny among the stars. Furthermore, participation in the grand march of progress isn't optional; once the direction of forward movement is determined, everyone is expected to join in the march, and those who show insufficient enthusiasm can expect to be driven forward by whatever means are at hand.

That same logic pervades Faustian culture at all levels. Have you noticed how common it is, for example, for people who come up with a diet that's good for their health to insist to all and sundry that the same diet must be good for everyone's health, that every other diet is bad and evil and wrong, and that if only everyone can be browbeaten into following the one true diet, all illness will go away? It's the identical Faustian tune, transposed into the key of crank nutrition. The food crackpot seeks to occupy the culturally mandated role of the bright individual with the "Aha!" moment that changes everything, so that the one true diet can become the fixed direction along which dietary progress can then march onward forever. More generally, within the worldview of Faustian cultures, any good idea must be good for all people, and those who don't accept it voluntarily must be forced to comply.

It's when these efforts at forced compliance fail and the onward march of progress falls flat on its face, in turn, that the downside of the Faustian narrative becomes painfully clear, because it has no way to deal with failure. That's something that varies dramatically from one great culture to another. The Chinese and Indian great cultures, for example, differ in immensely important ways but approach time and change through a broadly similar scheme: a vision of cyclic movement. Hindu philosophy has one of the two most richly elaborated schemes of cyclic time in any recorded high culture—its only rival is the equally intricate system of nested cycles worked out by the great cultures of native Mesoamerica. In both these traditions, everything that happens has happened countless times before and will happen countless times again, and if hard times come, why, that's just another incident in the spinning of time's vast wheel.

The Chinese vision of time is different, but equally cyclical. The I Ching, the great Chinese textbook of time theory, identifies sixty-four basic conditions of time, each of which can morph into any of the others by way of specific transformations. Thus the rise and fall of nations and dynasties isn't fixed quite so rigidly as in India or Mesoamerica. A government that pays attention to the way that time is flowing can often prevent the conditions of downfall from coming into play—in traditional Chinese terms, to keep hold of the mandate of Heaven and prevent it from shifting to new hands. In the Chinese way of seeing things, in turn, when hard times come, that just means that the bureaucrats in the capital have failed to judge the temporal flux correctly, and the situation will be rectified just as soon as the bureaucrats either get a clue or have their heads displayed on bamboo spears by the soldiers of the incoming dynasty.

The Magian culture doesn't have a cyclical sense of time—there's no other great culture that has had a so strictly linear vision of history—but the inherent flexibility of the Magian temporal scheme makes it relatively easy to deal with failure and defeat. In the Magian world-view, after all, the community of the faithful is constantly besieged by the powers of evil, which are permitted great leeway by the one true God for His inscrutable reasons. Someday the Messiah or Christ or the Mahdi or whoever will show up and transform the world utterly, but no one knows when, and in the meantime the faithful must expect to have their faith tried in the flames of worldly disappointment and suffering.

The Apollonian great culture had none of these resources to hand. In the Apollonian vision of history, again, once the universe is set in order by the might of its rightful ruler, and everyone accepts their proper place in the order of things, that's the way it's supposed to stay forever. The fall of the Roman Empire was thus a shattering experience for those who lived through its more drastic phases. A strong case can be made—and indeed it was made, early in the fifth century CE, by Augustine of Hippo in his polemic masterpiece *The City of God*—that the fall of Rome disproved the basic assumptions of the Apollonian worldview. That was what left the field clear for the rising Magian culture to seize the imagination of the ancient world and impose its own religious and cultural vision on the disillusioned masses of the late Roman world.

The Faustian culture, though, is even more vulnerable to the same sort of disillusionment. If we were to set up a spectrum of resilience to the experience of failure among great cultures, with India and China way over to one end of the spectrum, Faustian culture is about as far as you can go to the other end. For the Faustian sense of time to remain intact, after all, it's not enough to survive; it's not even enough to establish the sort of steady state to which Apollonian culture aspired, and which it achieved for centuries at a time. The Faustian sense of time requires progress—continued movement in the same direction. When that movement stops, or even slows down noticeably, the widening gap between what's supposed to happen and what's actually happening becomes a source of massive cognitive dissonance, and if that condition keeps going for more than a little while, people start to wig out.

In the end, that's what lies behind the cascading absurdities of the U.S. political mainstream today. In the early 1980s, a set of economic policies—among them, free-trade agreements, tacit encouragement of unlimited illegal immigration, and ever-expanding government regulations that benefited big corporations at the expense of small businesses—got assigned the role of the fixed direction that economic progress would thereafter follow. About a decade later, the Rescue Game, with its allotment of the roles of "victim" and "persecutor" by gender and ethnicity and its systematic erasure of the realities of class interest and class prejudice, got assigned the same status in terms of social and cultural progress.

Both the policies and the ideology failed to achieve their ostensible goal: neither the general prosperity that was supposed to result from the former nor the increasing equality that was supposed to come out of the latter ever got around to showing up. The result, as we've seen, was a forceful backlash, spearheaded by those who were expected to carry the costs of both the policies and the ideology while receiving none of the benefits. In 2016 the backlash put opponents of the policies and the ideology alike into decisive positions in the executive and judicial branches of the U.S. government, and the economic boom that free-trade policies were supposed to provide was set in motion by the abolition of free-trade policies.

In response, the defenders of yesterday's version of progress did what failed causes normally do in a Faustian society: they reverted to the habits of the Magian pseudomorphosis. Thus you get the radical moral dualism, the posturing as goodness incarnate, the increasingly shrill insistence that the backlash against their version of progress can only be motivated by deliberate evil, the claims that the end of the world will follow promptly now that the self-anointed Good People have failed. If supporters of Donald Trump know their way around the history of ideas, they're watching these antics with glee, since—as noted above—such diatribes show that the movement whose followers resort to them is on its last legs.

Keep in mind, though, that the antics we're seeing in U.S. politics today are a mild preview of the far more drastic disillusionment that's already beginning to take shape as the entire Faustian project of perpetual progress betrays the hopes that have been placed on it. The difficulty that Faustian culture has never grasped is that any attempt at continued movement in the same direction is subject to the law of diminishing returns. Scientific discovery and technological progress aren't exempt from this law; it's worth noting that the cost of each generation of scientific and technological advances has increased steadily with each passing decade, while the benefits provided by each decade's advances, on average, has turned out to be more and more marginal where it hasn't yet dipped well into negative numbers.

We're already seeing people going back to an earlier generation of cell phones because the latest gimmick-laden smartphones are literally more trouble than they're worth, and vinyl records and printed books are coming back into fashion years after they were supposedly outmoded by fancier but less satisfactory technologies. In the same way, manned space flight has become a publicity stunt practiced by ambitious nations and billionaire celebrities, rather than the inevitable next leap forward it was supposed to become by now.

The narrative of human expansion into outer space is perhaps the most typically Faustian of all our dreams, the ultimate expression of a culture that loves to imagine itself zooming out to infinity in all directions. Scientists have known for decades that space colonization is never going to happen: outside Earth's magnetosphere, space is so full of hard radiation that prolonged exposure to it will guarantee death by radiation poisoning, and neither the Moon nor Mars nor any other body in the solar system that human beings can visit has a magnetosphere like Earth's, strong enough to keep out the lethal rays that stream from the gigantic unshielded nuclear reactor at the center of the solar system. The continuing hold of the myth of space colonization on our collective imagination, in the teeth of such hard scientific details, may turn out to be the weak point that brings the whole grandiose dream of perpetual progress crashing down. If it's not that, though, it'll be something else.

If the future doesn't consist of the grand march of humanity to some high destiny among the stars, though, what then? That is the great question of the century ahead of us, and the most likely answer—the one that other civilizations have found as their own overblown dreams popped or slowly deflated—is a future of reassessment and recovery. In our case, one of the great driving forces behind that future will be the recognition, already dawning in many minds, that the rush to progress has replaced successful technologies with things that don't work as well, or at all. More and more people are already turning their backs on the latest dysfunctional upgrades and new-but-emphatically-not-improved technotrinkets to return to things that actually work. Meanwhile an assortment of pseudomorphoses are beginning to break down as the waning charisma of Faustian culture gives way to a renewed appreciation of the value of older cultural visions. Expect world-class meltdowns as that reality begins to sink in.

In the Faustian worldview, after all, it's inconceivable that the world's cultures each have their own possibilities, their own values and insights and ways of understanding the world, which cannot be reduced to any single trajectory. In the Faustian worldview, there is only one range of valid possibilities open to human beings, the one embraced and partly exemplified by Faustian cultures. All other cultures can be seen only as inadequate attempts to attain the Faustian model. There can be no different but equally valid sets of values and insights and ways of understanding the world; there is simply the Faustian way, which is self-evidently true, and every other way, which is superstitious, benighted, and obviously wrong.

In exactly the same way, it's unthinkable to the Faustian mind that history might consist of a sequence of different trajectories of rise and fall. There is only one trajectory, the one that begins in the squalor and ignorance of the caves, fumbles its way through various cultural forms that can be judged and found wanting on the basis of their difference from ours, and then finally figures out the one true way of progress and goes soaring confidently upward toward its supposedly inevitable destiny out there among the stars. Thus it's not at all surprising that Spengler's ideas reliably generate the same sort of nervous laughter followed by angry pushback that you'll get if you point out, among a group of middle-aged people frantically trying to cling to the waning phantasm of youth, that every one of them will soon grow old and die.

The difficulty faced right now by true believers in the Faustian vision, in turn, is precisely that the world no longer caters to their dreams. While a few narrow fields of technology continue to advance, having not yet finished working through their finite range of possibilities, most of the artifacts of contemporary life in the Western world follow patterns laid down for a century or more. Meanwhile a pervasive decline in real standards of living has been under way for decades, and some of the most heavily ballyhooed triumphs of the recent past are already slipping quietly out of reach.

All the recent rehashes of the typical future-fantasies of the mid-twentieth century—the faux-confident chatter about space travel, flying cars, robots replacing human jobs and the like, which featured so heavily in the comic books and pulp entertainment of my childhood in the 1960s—thus can be seen as the cultural equivalents of comb-overs, face-lifts, Viagra, and Botox, the increasingly frantic attempts of the aging to cling to the scraps of a youth they no longer possess and pretend that old age is solely for other people. It's the same motive, covert but powerful, that leads universities in the United States to turn away from the study of the artistic and cultural heritage of Western civilization: compare these to their epigones in the present or recent past, and it's painfully clear just how absurd it is to insist that Andy Warhol and

John Cage—much less their current replacements—represent any sort of advance over, let's say, Rembrandt and Bach.

Thus I expect Faustian culture to undergo the same kind of disillusionment that swept the Apollonian worldview into history's dustbin. If anything, to judge by the foreshocks of that event that followed Donald Trump's 2016 election, the rejection of the myth of progress may be even more sudden and sweeping. That won't necessarily involve the collapse of nations—I expect that, too, but it'll happen later on, as a result of other pressures—but it's certain to involve the overthrow of most of the assumptions that govern public policies and personal lives alike just now. Many of my readers have already been through the tectonic shift that follows when it really sinks in that the future isn't going to be better than the present. The rest of you might want to brace yourselves, since you'll be having the same experience soon enough.

Get beyond the facile insistence that the grand march of progress is still plodding away toward the stars, and Spengler's vision offers a more meaningful way to make sense of the far future. He holds up the past as a mirror in which the future can be glimpsed: a future marked, across the Western world, by the exhaustion of creative potentials; the winnowing of the past to produce an enduring canon of scientific, literary, and artistic achievements; the coming of irreversible economic and political decline, and the rest.

On the far side of that trajectory lies the emergence of new cultures with their own values and insights and ways of understanding the world. As I've already suggested, two of these will likely emerge in parallel borderland regions to east and west of Faustian culture's European homeland: in European Russia, and in particular in the Volga river basin; and in eastern North America, and in particular in the Ohio River basin and the Great Lakes littoral. To my mind, it's worth thinking about these, and trying to glimpse the shapes of these unborn great cultures.

There are remarkable parallels between America and Russia, balanced by equally important differences. Let's start with the parallels. Both came into being in the borderlands, where expanding Faustian nations confronted tribal cultures with much simpler technologies and much more stable relationships to the natural world. The native peoples of North America and Siberia are related genetically and culturally by way of the vanished Bering land bridge, and they had similar impacts on the expanding cultures that partly erased them and partly absorbed them. What's more, the experience of the frontier, the encounter with vast spaces inconceivably larger than anything the limited horizons of Europe could offer, shaped Russian and American cultures in similar ways.

Yet a crucial difference marks these two encounters, and the broader histories in which they have so important a place: a difference of time. Russia's great era of frontier expansion took place in the sixteenth and seventeenth centuries, while America's took place in the eighteenth and nineteenth centuries. More generally, Russia has been a coherent cultural entity much longer than English-speaking North America has. Russia is old enough to have had its first pseudomorphosis from the Magian culture of the Middle East by way of Byzantium, and got its second from the Faustian culture of western Europe right about the time that the European colonies on the Atlantic coast were first getting past the subsistence stage. America, by contrast, is still in the waning days of its first pseudomorphosis, and has some centuries to go before a second pseudomorphosis kickstarts the emergence of its own unique cultural forms.

That difference of time is mapped onto a wider difference, which has to do with place. One of the things that Spengler's analysis stresses—and one of the aspects of his work that tends to offend Faustian sensibilities most strongly—is the way that specific great cultures are bound to specific regions of the world, and never quite manage to transplant themselves successfully to other lands. The home ground of Faustian culture is western and central Europe, as already noted, and whenever it has established its cultural forms or political control outside that region, the result is inevitably a layer of Faustian elite culture over the top of a very different cultural substrate. You can see this at work in both the protocultures we're discussing. In New York and Saint Petersburg, the intelligentsia and the privileged classes go through the motions of European culture. Meanwhile, away from the centers of power, in farm towns along the banks of the Ohio and the Volga, the European veneer is very thin where it exists at all, and something rooted far more deeply in the soil and the soul of the countryside comes close to the surface.

Vine Deloria Jr.'s *God Is Red* is a crucial resource here, too, as it's one of the few works in any modern Western language to grasp the profound spiritual importance of place. Magian culture understood that implicitly—notice how Magian religions inevitably orient themselves toward specific, geographically unique centers of pilgrimage—but Faustian culture can't grasp it at all. To the Faustian mind, the landscape is a blank slate waiting to be overwritten by the will of the heroic individual whose deeds are the bread and butter of Faustian mythmaking. Note the way that Faustian cultures prefer to talk, not of place, but of space: not of localities with their own character and qualities, but of emptiness that, at least in our imagination, can be put to whatever sequence of temporary uses we happen to have in mind.

Every culture has its blind spots, and this is one of ours. Carl Jung, while traveling in America, happened to see workers streaming out of a factory. To his European eye, many members of the crowd looked distinctly Native American, and he was startled when his host insisted there was probably not one Native American there. Both men were correct. The land—any land—puts its stamp on the bodies, the actions, and the thoughts of the people who are born and raised there. The American who tries to be European has been a butt of edged humor in Europe for centuries now, because the result always rings false to European ears. Exactly the same thing is true of the Europeanized Russian, though the details of the mismatch are different, since the Russian bears the imprint of a different land.

It's because of this imprint, reflected in details of history and culture, that it's possible to glimpse a little of the shape of the two great cultures we're discussing. Each great culture throughout history, Spengler showed, has what amounts to a distinctive theme, a core concept from which that culture extracts the problems it considers important and unfolds the resources it will direct to their solution. Understand that theme and you understand crucial elements of the great culture that will pick it up, and eventually run it into the ground.

The central theme of Faustian culture is infinite expansion. That's why any Faustian thinker who comes up with a new political cause or a new diet instantly assumes that everyone, everywhere ought to embrace the cause or take up the diet; that's why so much of our technological prowess has focused obsessively on the quest to erase distance; that's why the word *freedom* in Faustian terms always ends up being defined as freedom to follow the one right path, and to bully other people into following it too. From square-rigged ships to trains to cars to airplanes to rockets, from semaphore to telegraphy to radio to television to the internet, it's all about extending a straight line to infinity, which is after all not surprising in the only culture in history to use linear perspective in its art.

Compare that to Magian culture, the great culture that rose, ripened, and settled into its enduring forms many centuries earlier in the Middle East. The central theme of Magian culture is the relationship between the human community and God. Where Faustian culture faces outward toward infinite space, Magian culture turns inward, forming an attentive circle around a unique human being whose words and deeds communicate an equally unique revelation from on high. Think of Jesus in the midst of his apostles, or Muhammad in the midst of his companions, and you've got the basic image.

That's reflected just as clearly in such classic products of the Magian pseudomorphosis as the Arthurian legends, with Arthur in the midst of his knights as a lightly secularized reflection of the theme. Even there, you can catch the first stirrings of the Faustian spirit: Arthur ends his days, not in a tomb that serves as a site of pilgrimage—the usual destiny of the Magian central figure—but vanishing into the unknown distance across the western sea. "Not wise the thought, a grave for Arthur," says an old Welsh text, and Tennyson echoes the same theme a thousand years later: "From the great deep to the great deep he goes."

Those of my readers who are interested in the subject can find the basic themes of past and present great cultures discussed at great length in Spengler's *The Decline of the West*. Let's turn toward the future, though, and try to grasp what we can of the central themes of the Russian and American great cultures to come.

A caveat is of course needed here. I'm not Russian; my sole exposure to Russian culture comes from three years of high school classes in the Russian language, followed by a fair bit of sympathetic reading in Russian literature and history. I've never been to Russia, and whatever whispers come with the winds off the great Eurasian steppes to the Volga valley are outside my experience. Fortunately there have been a good number of thoughtful Russian writers who've grappled with the question of the shape of a future Russian great culture, and their take is that its central theme is best described by a term that has no exact equivalent in English: *sobornost*.

If I understand the concept—and I'll happily accept correction from Russian readers if I don't—*sobornost* is a collective identity that arises out of shared experience and shared history. It's not defined from above, like the doctrine handed down to the community of the faithful that provides Magian culture with its basic theme. Rather, it ripens organically in individual lives, as the natural fulfillment of individual identity. In a culture of *sobornost,* what lies at the heart of each person is not some unique essence, but a link with the whole. It's for this reason that traditional Russian villages were arranged in a series of concentric circles with a holy place at the center, houses around that, gardens around that, fields further out, and the forest sweeping away into the distance beyond. Each part of the village has its place in a pattern that makes it formally equal with the others.

The first stirrings of the American great culture are fainter at this point—not surprising, as its flowering will be quite a bit further in the future, and we have a second pseudomorphosis to get through first. One measure of that faintness is that there isn't yet a good clear English word for the theme that already differentiates American culture from those of other societies. Since the land keeps radiating its basic influence while peoples come and go, I'll borrow a term from Chinook jargon—the old trade language of northwestern native North America, which was once spoken from northern California to Alaska and from the Pacific Ocean to the western edges of the Great Plains—and speak of *tamanous*.

Tamanous—that's pronounced tah-MAN-oh-oose, by the way—is the guardian spirit of the individual, and also his luck and his destiny. In a great many Native American cultures, finding and establishing a sacred relationship with one's *tamanous* is the primary religious act a person can engage in, an essential part of achieving adulthood, and something that most people do as a matter of course. The result is a religious vision unlike any other, in which the personal relationship between the individual and an equally unique and individualized spiritual power takes center stage.

I once had the privilege of attending a traditional religious ceremony at a Native American reservation north of Everett in Washington State. To the rolling thunder of drums, the participants—men and women of several related Coast Salish tribes—danced the dances of their *tamanous*. No two danced the same steps or made the same gestures; each, caught up by the power of the drums, expressed the nature of his or her own unique spiritual protector and the gifts it brought. That's the traditional religion of the Salish—not a collective relationship with a single overarching power or a well-organized pantheon, but a dazzling diversity of individual relationships with spiritual beings, none of which has any necessary relevance to anyone but the human and the spirit who share in it. Similar patterns can be found in many other Native American cultures.

Look at the history of American religion since European settlement and you can see this same pattern taking shape out of the last scraps of the Magian pseudomorphosis. In traditional Christianity, the individual is a part of the universal Body of Christ that is the church, united by a shared doctrine and praxis. In America, even in Colonial times, that began to break down, to be replaced by a focus on the individual relationship with Jesus and personal insight into the meaning of Scripture. It's the homegrown American versions of Christianity that call believers to take Jesus as their personal savior, through a process of personal transformation that, as one generation gives way to another, comes more and more to resemble a Christian vision quest—and is there really that much difference between a personal savior and a *tamanous*?

More generally, the fault lines that divide the first stirrings of a distinctively American culture from the Faustian culture of the West all involve conflicts between individual liberty and the will to power that pervades the Faustian mind. The mythic narratives of Faustian culture, as already noted, all revolve around the conflict between the visionary individual who knows the truth, and the ignorant and superstitious masses who must be forced to accept it.

Where Faustian pseudomorphoses hold sway, as in Russia and America, that reliably helps drive the rise of an intelligentsia of the kind discussed earlier in this chapter, who try to bribe, bully, and browbeat the recalcitrant populace into accepting the latest fashionable ideology. Combine the Faustian will to infinite extension with the class issues discussed at length earlier in this book, and it's easy to understand that whenever members of a Faustian-influenced intelligentsia start by insisting that people should be free to do something, they end up trying either to coerce everyone into doing it, to punish anyone who suggests alternatives to it, or both. Those readers who pay attention to the news will have no difficulty thinking of examples.

In Russia for centuries now, such projects have run face first into the brick wall of *sobornost,* the patient and maddeningly irrefutable collective identity that shrugs off alien ideas in order to return to its own enduring patterns. If Spengler and the Russian thinkers mentioned earlier are correct, the time of the Faustian pseudomorphosis in Russia is drawing to a close, and the next century or so will see a newborn Russian great culture shake off or radically repurpose the cultural inheritance of Europe in the service of a wholly different vision of humanity and the cosmos, in which *sobornost* will emerge as a central theme.

And America? We've got longer to go, and another pseudomorphosis to get through. Even so, the stirrings of the future American great culture can be tracked in our own time, as an intelligentsia with its head full of Faustian notions collides with a vision of humanity and the cosmos that's just as frustratingly different as anything to be found on Russian soil. To those who want to claim the role of visionary individual revealing the truth to the deplorable masses, the masses increasingly often are saying, "If that's your truth, hey, by all means follow it. It's not ours"—and "ours," in turn, breaks up on closer examination into a crowd of dancing figures, no two of whom are taking the same steps or making the same gestures.

There is a different right way for each individual. That's the message, or one part of the message, that the American land has been whispering to its human residents for a very long time. It's not a message for everyone in the world—again, each great culture has its own theme, and the core theme of the future American great culture is no more universal than any other. I suspect that a thousand years from now, the incommensurability between *sobornost* and *tamanous* will become the same kind of massive political fact that the conflict between Magian and Faustian cultures was in the year 1600 or so. In the meantime, though, that message deserves attention here, because it has had an immense and generally unrecognized impact on the politics of our own day.

7

The Tatters of the King
Magic and Power in Post-Trump America

He spoke of Cassilda and Camilla, and sounded the cloudy depths of Demhe, and the Lake of Hali. "The scalloped tatters of the King in Yellow must hide Yhtill forever," he muttered, but I do not believe Vance heard him. Then by degrees he led Vance along the ramifications of the Imperial family, from Naotalba and the Phantom of Truth, to Aldones, and then tossing aside his manuscript and notes, he began the wonderful story of the Last King.

FROM "THE REPAIRER OF REPUTATIONS"
IN *THE KING IN YELLOW*

L et's pause now to draw together the varied threads we've been following so far, and bring the improbable events of the last few years of American history into a tentative focus. When Donald Trump declared himself as a candidate for the presidency in 2015, he did so in a nation riven by dissensions that no one in the corporate mass media or the comfortable classes was willing to discuss at all. On the obvious surface level, the most important of these was the chasm between what I've termed the salary class and the wage class. That chasm had a straightforward cause: for more than four decades the salary class pushed policies that drove the wage class ever further into poverty and misery, while insisting that this stark fact could not be discussed openly in the media or in any public forum.

A breathtaking degree of magical thinking went into defending this state of affairs and insisting that there was no alternative to it. Economists babbled enthusiastically about how globalization and open borders would bring prosperity to the wage class while the wage class was being impoverished by globalization and open borders. Politicians and pundits insisted that people in the wage class, who were left penniless by the offshoring of jobs and the mass hiring of illegal immigrants at starvation wages, should go to college at their own expense (or that of the taxpaying public) to get training for jobs that either didn't exist in the first place, or were promptly offshored in their turn. More broadly, long before Hillary Clinton made the word *deplorable* fashionable, a great many members of the salary class took up the convenient habits of vilifying the wage class for its failure to follow salary-class fashions, and blaming it for its own impoverishment and immiseration. All these were magical actions—attempts to cause changes in consciousness in accordance with will—and they and their effects were maintained by incantations and spells in which the ritual drama of the Rescue Game played an important role.

The chasm between the salary class and the wage class that was defended by these magical workings was not limited to straightforward economics, though. It reached down into deep cultural strata where very few American intellectuals have been willing to follow it. It traced out a schism in the American soul that has been a potent political fact since Colonial times—the line of division between the wealthy cosmopolitan cultures of the coastal urban enclaves and the impoverished and fiercely local rural cultures of the American hinterland. Deeper still, where the chasm plunged into bedrock, it divided the veneer of European culture prized by America's comfortable classes, and promoted and defended by the American intelligentsia, from the first inchoate stirrings of a culture not yet born, which will be rooted in the American land, and develop along principles inconceivable to the European mind.

These were the divisions that made the rise of Donald Trump inevitable—or rather, that made the rise of someone like Donald Trump inevitable. No historical necessity required the cause of ordinary deplorable Americans in the flyover states to be championed by a brash and blustering New York real estate mogul who'd taken up a second career as a wrestling promoter and a third as a reality television star. Anyone with the charisma, connections, and personal wealth to make a run at the presidency could have done the same thing Trump did—but someone was going to do it sooner or later. Trump happened to be the person who got swept up in this particular tide and carried by it to an improbable destiny.

In exactly the same way, no historical necessity required the cadres of disaffected youth who rallied around Trump's cause to turn to chaos magic as their preferred weapon of political warfare, any more than it was inevitable that they should raise the banner of a cartoon frog or turn an otherwise forgettable Europop song into their anthem. Once the American establishment embraced the common elite tactic of educating far more young people for managerial jobs than the job market could take, those cadres of disaffected youth were certain to emerge, and once a Trumpesque figure rose up and called them to arms, they were just as certain to answer: in the *Sturm und Drang* of Oswald Spengler's language, that was Destiny, not Incident. Even so, the cadres could have turned to political organization, or to revolutionary violence, or to any of the many other instruments of political action that lay to hand. It was Incident that they turned to magic, and so wrote an uncanny chapter in the history of our time.

Physicists point out that on the quantum level, a particle exists solely as a diffuse probability wave until someone observes it. Once that act of observation happens, the probability wave collapses and there the particle is, locked into some specific position and trajectory from which all its future actions must unfold. This same principle applies in the political sphere. Until Trump became the standard-bearer of the wage class and the great opponent of the Faustian pseudomorphosis at this stage of American history, and a gallimaufry of newly minted alt-right chaos mages brandishing savagely funny internet memes rose up to support his candidacy under the banner of an Egyptian frog god, anything could have happened.

At this point, though, the probability wave has collapsed, and events have set into a position and trajectory from which the future is unfolding. One clear demonstration of that change is the triumph of Boris Johnson and the Conservative party in the 2019 British general election. For decades now, since Tony Blair's New Labour movement supplanted Margaret Thatcher's hardline conservatism, Britain was locked into the same cross-party consensus as the United States: all parties pandered to the salary class at the expense of the wage class, and backed the same policies of economic globalization, open borders, and metastatic regulation that drove the American wage class into destitution, with similar effect on the British wage class.

Johnson is, for all practical purposes, Britain's Donald Trump, fully kitted out with the brash personality, the shoot-from-the-hip verbal style, the unfashionable hairstyle, and the rest. More to the point, though, Johnson's entire approach to the 2019 election was clearly designed to copy Donald Trump's 2016 electoral strategy. Brexit—Britain's exit from the European Union, which had been voted by a national referendum in 2016, and stonewalled thereafter by the political elite—made a convenient battering ram for that purpose, as it was supported by crucial sectors of the wage class in perennial Labour strongholds in the Midlands and North, and most strongly opposed by salary class sectors that weren't going to vote Conservative anyway. Johnson's victory thus marks the point at which what we may as well call Trumpism—the shotgun wedding of wage-class populism and conservative nationalism—came of age.

It's in this context that the outcome of the 2020 U.S. election needs to be understood. In the election campaign, the salary class and the corporate mass media pulled out all the stops, tried every trick they could think of, exploited the coronavirus epidemic and every other turn of events that came their way, and still barely pulled off a paper-thin victory against Trump. Both parties went into the election expecting a decisive result—the Democrats hoping to sweep Trump away and seize control of the Senate, the Republicans hoping to see Trump reelected with a strong mandate and seize control of the House—and for all practical purposes, both parties lost. Democratic politicians gamely tried to claim a mandate for their geriatric candidate, without convincing anybody. For the next two years at least, the United States can expect a bitter stalemate between salary-class and wage-class interests.

From the magical perspective, however, the most important point about the 2020 election was that the high strangeness that shaped the 2016 election failed to put in an appearance. The torrent of "gets" and other synchronicities that heralded Trump's election did not show up to herald his reelection, and the 2020 campaign turned into yet another slanging match between politicians, marred (as close elections in the United States are always marred) by more or less credible claims of vote fraud, highlighting the schisms within a bitterly divided nation and offering little hope for a resolution on any terms at all. One possible cause of the resulting mess is that the contending mages of the alt-right and the Magic Resistance set out to make the other side lose, and both succeeded. It seems at least as likely, however, that the archetypal forces that drove the Trump phenomenon in 2016 had no need for a second Trump term.

As I write these words, Biden and his spokespeople are busy mouthing the usual words about uniting the nation and coming together. We don't yet know whether that will turn out to be just another set of empty noises covering a headlong flight back to the failed past of neoliberal economics and neoconservative foreign policy, or whether the circle of Obama-era political and corporate flacks surrounding Biden has learned something from the events of the past five years and will quietly moderate those policies in order to mollify the wage class. It's possible, if Biden and his handlers are more capable than they've shown any sign of being, that the stalemate in national politics might turn into a breathing space in which the first movements toward viable compromise might take place. It's just as possible, if Biden and his handlers fumble things badly enough, that a great many wage-class Americans could lose faith entirely in the democratic process and turn to terrorism or domestic insurgency instead, plunging the nation into a long nightmare of violence and economic collapse. It's still too early to say.

That said, a change of high importance has already begun to reshape the politics of the industrial world: the destruction of the wage class discussed in this book is being talked about openly in a growing number of blogs and websites. It's too early yet to be certain, but it looks as though the web of political sorcery and cultural taboo that shut out the interests of the wage class from the collective conversation of our time has broken down irrevocably. It may well be this is the goal that the archetypal forces sought.

And magic? It will continue to be studied and practiced in twenty-first-century America as it has been in every other age and society. The fulminations of rationalist pseudoskeptics and professionally angry atheists have had no measurable effect on the flourishing of occult studies over the last four decades, and there is no reason to think that they will have any more effect over the decades ahead. As long as our society remains divided into the excluded and the excluders—and it bears remembering that this is the normal condition of any complex society—the excluded will keep practicing magic to cope with the dysfunctions of their society, and the excluders will keep practicing magic to convince themselves that the dysfunctions don't exist.

What remains uncertain is whether magic will remain as central to the political discourse of our time as it was during the era of Trump. If the Biden administration can somehow find or make a middle ground where the shrill rage of the salary class and the silent fury of the wage class can be muted to some degree, and the compromise that is an essential element of democratic governance again becomes an option, then it's possible that magic will move into the background of politics again, at least for a time. If the Biden administration stumbles hard and sends the United States plunging into a decade or so of homegrown terrorism or domestic insurgency, magic will move into the background then as well, leaving the ground clear for the harsher language of violence to settle the matter.

If the future unfolds between these two extremes, however, magic is likely to retain an important role in the politics of the near future. Now that the spell of silence surrounding the systematic impoverishment and immiseration of the wage class has been broken, new spells will be cast by all sides, and the methods involved are unlikely to be limited to the manipulative magic that Ioan Couliano anatomized, practiced, and died for. We have entered a liminal space in which even the most basic assumptions about our collective destiny are up for grabs, and strange bright banners of destiny are already being unfurled, leading in directions no one has yet begun to explore. In terms of the metaphor central to this book, we have all seen the Orange Sign, and there is no way back from that moment of revelation.

What makes this revelation all the more mordant is that the mass tantrum of America's mass media, intelligentsia, and comfortable classes that got started with Trump's election and has raged ever since was described right down to the small details in the 1970s by pioneering grief researcher Elisabeth Kübler-Ross. Granted, she was talking about the five psychological stages that people go through when coming to terms with the reality of a terminal illness, but it makes an accurate model for what we may as well call the five stages of Donald Trump.

The first stage, of course, is denial: as Kübler-Ross describes it, the stunned refusal to admit that what's happened has actually happened. Think of the widespread fixation among Democrats in 2016 on the popular-vote totals, the insistence that it was all a mere fluke or must have been rigged by the Russians, the public figures who loudly announced that they would never utter the phrase "President Trump," the transformation of "Not my president" into a woke mantra, and so on. All this was a futile attempt to deny the fact that the American people, according to the rules set out by the Constitution, had ignored the demands of the privileged classes and elected Donald Trump as the 45th president of the United States.

The second stage is anger: in Kübler-Ross's description, blind unreasoning rage kindled by the sudden appearance of a yawning gap between expectations and reality. Here again, no one who had any contact with the mass media or the privileged strata of American society can have missed the torrents of rage poured out, not only at Trump himself, but at anything and everything that could conceivably be connected or associated or lumped together with him. Anger, according to occult teachings about personality, is a secondary emotion, something we feel because it's easier than feeling fear or shame or grief, and this was a fine example of that in action. Beneath the outpouring of blind rage against Trump and all his works was the terror of a privileged class suddenly confronted with the waning of its influence.

The third stage is bargaining. It's important not to misunderstand this stage, as the bargains in question aren't made with whatever has kickstarted the process. In Kübler-Ross's writings, this is the stage at which terminally ill people repent their sins and make sweeping promises to God or their family or their doctor. The bargaining stage in the present case had plenty of manifestations. The Mueller report and the impeachment hearings in the House of Representatives were among the high points of this stage, but bargaining reached its peak with the 2020 presidential campaign. The bargain that millions of Americans tried to make with the universe in that election was this: if we vote Trump out, then the universe will take away the entire phenomenon he represents, the rise of the populism of the deplorables.

The fourth stage is depression. We haven't gotten there yet, though I suspect that it's very close. Donald Trump himself is the chief obstacle to this stage, because it won't be until he leaves the political scene, and the populist movement he spearheaded remains lively and active, that the last scraps of the magic of the excluders will begin to crack apart.

In an important sense, Trump was as necessary to the salary class as he was to the wage class. While he was the center of American political discourse, it was possible to pretend that the status quo of the pre-Trump era was just fine for everyone until the awful orange man came along and wrecked it. In the aftermath of Trump's departure from power, as a new generation of populist politicians and activists pick up the same themes he rode to the White House and use them to belabor the salary class, that fiction will no longer be sustainable.

Off in the distance, finally, is the fifth stage, which is acceptance. Here again, it's important not to misunderstand this stage. Acceptance doesn't mean you have to like what's happened. Acceptance means dealing with the fact that it's not going to go away just because you don't like it. It's the process of coming to terms with the fact that the world has changed, and it has a payoff that none of the other stages have: it allows you to do something meaningful about the new reality. If you have a terminal illness, acceptance allows you to make arrangements that will allow you to die with some degree of dignity and ensure that your estate is settled the way you want it. If you're dealing with a new political reality, acceptance allows you to find your feet again and figure out how to offer the voters what they want, instead of what you want them to want or believe they ought to want.

We live in the opening stages of just such a new political reality in the United States today. Among the best measures of the rise of the new reality are the ongoing denunciations of "populism" in the mainstream media. What, pray tell, is populism? It's the political stance that says that the majority has the right to have a voice in the making of collective decisions. The opposite of populism, though you won't hear that mentioned in the denunciations I have in mind, is elitism: the viewpoint that only the self-proclaimed Good People have the right to a voice in decisions. That's a core feature of the ideology that's going to bits just now.

We can talk about the emergence of the new political reality in various ways, and I've explored some of them in this book. The one I'd like to consider as we sum up the reign of the King in Orange derives from the metaphor I've just used, the stages of grieving that Kübler-Ross discussed in her books. That is to say, we are talking about a death.

For precisely two hundred years before 2016, this country's political discourse was shaped—more powerfully, perhaps, than by any other single force—by the loose bundle of ideas, interests, and values that we can call American liberalism. That's the name on the toe tag we're examining. The most important trends shaping the political landscape of our time, to my mind, are the descent of the liberal movement into its final decadence, and the first stirrings of the postliberal politics that is already emerging in its wake.

To make sense of what American liberalism has been, what it has become, and what will happen in its aftermath, history is an essential resource. Ask a believer in a political ideology to define it, and you'll get one set of canned talking points; ask an opponent of that ideology to do the same thing, and you'll get another—and both of them will be shaped more by the demands of moment-by-moment politics than by any broader logic. Trace that ideology from its birth through its childhood, adolescence, adulthood, and descent into senility, and you get a better view of what it actually means.

Let's go back, then, to the wellsprings of the American liberal movement. Historians have argued for a good long time about the deeper roots of that movement, but its first visible upsurge can be traced to a few urban centers in the coastal Northeast in the years just after the War of 1812. Boston—nineteenth-century America's San Francisco—was the epicenter of the newborn movement, a bubbling cauldron of new social ideas to which aspiring intellectuals flocked from across the new Republic. Any of my readers who think that the naive and effervescent idealism of the 1960s was anything new in the American experience need to sit down with a copy of Nathaniel Hawthorne's *The Blithedale Romance,* which is set in the Massachusetts counterculture of the early nineteenth century—in fact, most of the action takes place on a commune. That's the context in which American liberalism was born.

From the very beginning, it was a movement of the educated elite. Though it spoke movingly about uplifting the downtrodden, the downtrodden themselves were permitted very little active part in it. It was also as closely intertwined with Protestant Christianity as the movement of the 1960s was with Asian religions; ministers from the Congregationalist and Unitarian churches played a central role in the movement throughout its early years, and the major organizations of the movement—the Anti-Slavery Societies, the Temperance League, and the Non-Resistant League, the first influential American pacifist group—were closely allied with churches, and staffed and supported by clergymen. Both the elitism and the Protestant Christian orientation, as we'll see, had a powerful influence on the way American liberalism evolved over the two centuries that followed.

Three major social issues formed the framework around which the new movement coalesced. The first was the abolition of slavery; the second was the prohibition of alcohol; the third was the improvement of the legal status of women. (The movement traversed a long and convoluted road before this latter goal took its ultimate form of legal and social equality between the sexes.) There were plenty of other issues that attracted their own share of attention from the movement—dietary reform, dress reform, pacifism, and the like—but all of them shared a common theme: the redefinition of politics as an expression of values.

Let's take a moment to unpack that last phrase. Politics at the time that American liberalism was born, as at most other periods in human history, was understood as a straightforward matter of interests—in the bluntest of terms, who got what benefits and who paid what costs. At that time, for example, one of the things that happened in the wake of every Presidential election is that the winner's party got to hand out federal jobs en masse to its supporters. It was called the "spoils system," as in "to the victor belongs the spoils;" people flocked to campaign for this or that presidential candidate as much in the hope of getting a comfortable federal job as for any other reason. Nobody saw anything wrong with that system, because politics was about interests.

In the same way, few people in the Constitutional Convention agonized over the ethics of the notorious provision that tacitly defined each slave as being 3/5ths of a person. I doubt the ethical side of the matter ever crossed many minds there, because politics was not about ethics—it was about interests—and the issue was simply one of finding a compromise that allowed each state to feel that its interests would be adequately represented in Congress. Values, in the thought of the time, belonged to church and to the private conscience of the individual; politics was about interests pure and simple.

(We probably need to stop here for a moment to deal with the standard response: "Yes, but they should have known better!" This is a classic example of a mistake we can call *chronocentrism.* Just as ethnocentrism privileges the beliefs, values, and interests of a particular ethnic group, chronocentrism does the same thing to the beliefs, values, and interests of a particular time. Chronocentrism is enormously common today, on all sides of the political and cultural landscape; you can see it when scientists insist that people in the Middle Ages should have known better than to believe in magic, for example, or when Christians insist that the old pagans should have known better than to believe in their many gods. In every case, it's simply one more attempt to evade the difficult task of understanding the past.)

Newborn American liberalism, though, rejected the division between politics and values. Their opposition to slavery, for example, had nothing to do with the divergent economic interests of the industrializing northern states and the plantation economy of the South, and everything to do with a devoutly held conviction that chattel slavery was morally wrong. Their opposition to alcohol, to the laws that denied civil rights to women, to war, and to everything else on the lengthy shopping list of the movement had to do with moral values, not with interests. That's where you see the impact of the movement's Protestant heritage: it took values out of the church and tried to apply them to the world as a whole. At the time, that was exotic enough that the moral crusades just mentioned got about as much political traction at the time as the colorful political and cultural fantasies of the 1960s did in their own day.

Both movements were saved from complete failure by the impact of war. The movement of the 1960s drew most of its influence on popular culture from its opposition to the Vietnam War, which is why it collapsed so completely when the war ended and the draft was repealed. The earlier movement had to wait a while for its war, and in the meantime it very nearly destroyed itself by leaping on board the same kind of apocalyptic fantasy that kicked the New Age movement into its current death spiral. In the late 1830s, frustrated by the failure of the perfect society to show up as quickly as they desired, a great many adherents of the new liberal movement embraced the prophecy of William Miller, a New England farmer who believed that he had worked out from the Bible the correct date of the Second Coming of Christ. When October 22, 1844, passed without incident, the resulting "Great Disappointment" was a body blow to the movement, and under other circumstances, could have led to its collapse, the way that the parallel failure of December 21, 2012, seems to be putting paid to the New Age movement.

By the time of the Great Disappointment, though, one of the moral crusades being pushed by American liberals had attracted the potent support of raw economic interest. The division between Northern and Southern states over the question of slavery was not primarily seen at the time as a matter of ethics, though of course northern politicians and media were quick to capitalize on the moral rhetoric of the Abolitionists. At issue was the shape of the nation's economic future. Was it going to be an agrarian society producing mostly raw materials for export, and fully integrated into a global economy centered on Britain—the Southern model? Or was it going to go its own way, raise trade barriers against the global economy, and develop its own industrial and agricultural economy for domestic consumption—the Northern model?

Such questions had immediate practical implications, because government policies that favored one model guaranteed the ruin of the other. Slavery was the linchpin of the Southern model, because the big Southern plantations required a vast supply of labor at next to no cost to turn a profit, and so slavery became a core issue targeted by Northern politicians and propagandists alike. Read detailed accounts of the struggles in Congress between northern and southern politicians, though, and you'll find that what was under debate had as much to do with trade policy and federal expenditures. Was there to be free trade, which benefited the South, or trade barriers, which benefited the North? Was the federal budget to pay for canals and roads, which benefited Northern interests by getting raw materials to factories and manufactured products to markets, but were irrelevant to Southern interests, which simply needed riverboats to ship cotton and tobacco to the nearest seaport?

Even the bitter struggles over which newly admitted states were to have slave-based economies, and which were not, had an overwhelming economic context in the politics of the time. The North wanted to see the western territories turned into a patchwork of family farms, producing agricultural products for the burgeoning cities of the eastern seaboard and the Great Lakes and buying manufactured goods from northern factories. The South wanted instead to see those same territories made available for plantations that would raise products for export to England and the world.

Yet the ethical dimension became central to Northern propaganda, as already noted, and that helped spread the liberal conviction that values as well as interests had a place in the political dialogue. By 1860, that conviction had become widespread enough that it even shaped thinking south of the Mason-Dixon Line. As originally written, for example, the second line of the Confederate song "The Bonny Blue Flag" ran "fighting for the property we won by honest toil"—and no one anywhere had any illusions about the skin color of the property in question. Before long, though, it was rewritten as "fighting for our liberty, with treasure, blood, and toil." The moment that change occurred, the South had already lost; it's possible to argue for slavery on grounds of crass economic interest, but once the focus of the conversation changes to values such as liberty, slavery becomes indefensible.

So the Civil War raged; the Confederacy rose and fell; the Northern economic model guided American economic policy for most of a century thereafter; and the liberal movement found its feet again. With slavery abolished, the other two primary goals took center stage, and the struggle to outlaw alcohol and get voting rights for women proceeded very nearly in lockstep. The 18th Amendment, prohibiting the manufacture and sale of alcohol in the United States, and the 19th Amendment, granting women the right to vote, were passed in 1919 and 1920 respectively, and even though Prohibition turned out to be a total flop, the same rhetoric was redirected toward drugs (legal in the United States until the 1930s) and continues to shape public policy today. Then came the Great Depression. With the election of Franklin Roosevelt in 1932—and even more so with his overwhelming reelection victory in 1936, when the GOP carried only two states—the liberal movement became the dominant force in American political life.

Triumph after triumph followed. The legalization of unions, the establishment of a tax-funded social safety net, the forced desegregation of the South: these and a galaxy of other reforms on the liberal shopping list duly took place. The remarkable thing is that all these achievements came about while the liberal movement was fighting opponents from both sides. To the right, of course, old-fashioned conservatives still dug in their heels and fought for the interests that mattered to them, but from the 1930s on, liberals also faced constant challenge from further left. American liberalism, as already mentioned, was a movement of the educated elite; it focused on helping the downtrodden rather than including them—and that approach increasingly ran into trouble as the downtrodden turned out to have ideas of their own that didn't have much to do with what liberals wanted to do for them.

Starting in the 1970s, in turn, American liberalism also ended up facing a third source of challenges—a new form of conservatism that borrowed the value-centered language of liberalism but used a different set of values to rally support to its cause: the values of conservative Protestant Christianity. In some ways, the rise of the so-called new conservatism with its talk about "family values" represented the final, ironic triumph of the long struggle to put values at the center of political discourse. By the 1980s, every political faction in American public life, no matter how grubby and venial its behavior and its goals, took care to festoon itself with some suitable collection of abstract values. That's still the case today: nobody talks about interests, even when interests are the obvious issue.

Thus you get the standard liberal response to criticism, which is to insist that the only reason anyone might possibly object to a liberal policy is because they have hateful values. That was the logic that underlay the strange phenomenon we explored at the beginning of this book, the frantic insistence by the mass media and the chattering classes that the people who voted for Donald Trump in 2016 could only have been motivated by racism, sexism, or some other currently unfashionable bigotry. It certainly couldn't have had anything to do with the way the salary class pursued its own interests at the expense of so many other people!

All this is reminiscent of a common theme in magical lore. Any number of hostile or tricksterish magical beings, from Rumpelstiltskin on down, depend for their power on the fact that nobody is able or willing to speak their names aloud. Do that, and all their spells and shenanigans dissolve like mist before a rising wind—and so all the efforts of such beings tend to go into making sure that nobody ever gets around to finding and speaking their names. That's a useful way of talking about the attempt to redefine the Trump phenomenon as anything but what it actually was: pushback from the classes that spent too much time on the losing end of the salary class's kleptocratic pursuit of its own economic advantage.

That is to say, American liberalism began its history with the insistence that values had a place in politics alongside interests, and ended its history using talk about values to silence discussion of the ways in which its members pursue their own interests. That's not a strategy with a long shelf life, because it rarely takes the other side more than a generation or two to identify and exploit the gap between rhetoric and reality. Once the clever girl in the fairy tale shouts "I know your name, it's Rumpelstiltskin!" the spell is broken—and the same is true of the spell of virtue signaling that the salary class has tried to weave in order to shield its pursuit of its own economic and political advantage from public criticism.

Ironies of this sort are anything but unusual in political history. It's astonishingly common for a movement that starts off trying to overturn the status quo in the name of some idealistic abstraction or other to check its ideals at the door once it becomes the status quo itself. If anything, American liberalism held onto its ideals longer than most and accomplished a great deal more than many. We all have reason to be grateful to that movement for ending such obvious abuses as slavery and the denial of civil rights to women, and for championing the idea that values as well as interests deserve a voice in the public sphere. We owe it the equivalent of a raised hat and a moment of silence, if no more, as American liberalism sinks into the decadence and final irrelevance that is the ultimate fate of every successful political movement.

Over the decades ahead, as a result of that process, we can expect to see dramatic shifts both in the platforms of the major parties, and the demographic groups that support each party. This is an ordinary event in political history—how many people these days remember that the Democratic Party, the party that backed the civil rights movement of the 1950s and 1960s, had been the pro-slavery party a hundred years earlier? Or that well into the twentieth century, Republicans supported environmental conservation and Democrats opposed it?

Exactly how the existing political landscape will shift is still an open question just now. Certainly the Democratic Party has no shortage of politicians and influential donors who remain committed to free trade, open borders, the regulatory state, and other policies that support the interests of the salary class, while the Republicans seem to be well on their way to becoming a populist party that supports protectionist trade policies, the enforcement of immigration laws, economic deregulation, and other policies that support the interests of the wage class. No doubt there will be repeated attempts on both sides to keep framing the issues in terms of values rather than interests, but I doubt those will succeed for long. Too many people have seen too clearly the way that the loudly touted values of both sides always end up pandering to the most blatant sort of material advantage.

The new political reality we face in today's America is thus one in which it's no longer possible to pretend that the only moral option is to give the salary class whatever it happens to want. That means, in turn, that members of the salary class who want something may just have to put up with the inconveniences of having to bargain for it, and offer members of other classes with some of the things they want, even when this inconveniences the salary class. It also means, as some of my readers may have noticed, that underprivileged groups who've been told to wait patiently for crumbs to fall from the table of the salary class are beginning to speak up for themselves and demand that their needs be taken into account now, thank you very much.

That is to say, we are returning to politics as usual. As the shrieks of denial and anger, the chatter of bargaining, and the moans of depression fall silent, what will eventually emerge is the normal processes of political life in a representative democracy, in which different sectors of the electorate offer their support to politicians in exchange for the policies they want and need, and politicians who don't follow through on their promises can expect to have the sectors that supported them turn to someone else next time around. What this shows, in turn, is that the period that came to an end in 2016 was a period of politics as *un*usual, in which the interests of a single class temporarily eclipsed the needs of everyone else.

In the longer run? These issues will fade and be replaced by others. It's a truism of history that no generation can successfully foresee the issues that will shape the political lives of its own grandchildren. If Spengler's correct—and the evidence so far is certainly in his favor—the great ideological conflicts of the last century or so don't have much of a shelf life left. In his theory, the rise of Caesarism, orange-colored or otherwise, marks the juncture at which personalities take over from ideologies as the driving force of Faustian political life. (It's entirely in keeping with history's wry sense of humor that in our case, this transformation should be heralded by the rise to power of one of the most over-the-top personalities of our time.)

None of this leaves any room in politics for the passionate Faustian faith in perpetual progress. As politics becomes personal rather than ideological, the claim that our collective life can be made perfect by building a better political mousetrap will be one of the early casualties. With it departs the paired delusions, so important to the political life of our recent past, that if only we can come up with the right system, everyone will behave the way that privileged intellectuals think they should behave, and that democracy can be defined as a system in which the majority always votes the way that these same privileged intellectuals tell them to vote.

And privilege itself? Of course it will continue to exist, in our society as in all others. Every human society without exception gives some members more say in making decisions than others. Since human beings are what they are, in turn, every human society without exception hands out those decision-making roles in ways that can reasonably be called unfair. That's true of all other species of social primates, too, so odds are it's as thoroughly hardwired into our behavioral repertoire as sex—or for that matter, hate.

The conventional wisdom on the Left nonetheless holds that it's not only possible but mandatory to create a society with no inequality at all, where everyone has the same privileges as affluent American liberals have today. The conventional wisdom on the right, by contrast, holds that existing inequalities are good and right and proper, and reflect the actual worth of the more or less privileged. Both are wrong, but they're wrong in different ways.

The Left's faith in the possibility of a society of perfect equality, where no one is more or less privileged than anybody else, has deep roots. Christian heretics in the Middle Ages roughed out the idea of a society in which perfect love would erase social divisions and everyone would share freely in all of life's blessings. Most of them had the great good sense to place this utopian vision on the far side of the Second Coming, when divine omnipotence could be counted on to take care of the practical difficulties of such a system. With the waning of Christian faith, Enlightenment *philosophes* such as Jean-Jacques Rousseau transposed the old vision into a new key, but lacked the perspicacity to find some existential barrier to shield the dream of a world of perfect equality from the fraught realities of human nature.

The result has been a long string of societies that proclaimed that they had abolished all privilege and made everyone equal. In every case, without exception, what happened instead was that an overt system of privilege was destroyed, and promptly replaced with a covert system of privilege—and since this latter was covert, it was much less subject to checks and balances, and much more likely to have to enforce its power via brute force rather than less grisly institutional pressures. That's why, from the Terror of revolutionary France to the killing fields of Cambodia, utopias of perfect equality so often end up awash in rivers of blood. On a less blood-spattered level, that's why the rhetoric of equality so widespread among contemporary American liberals has coexisted so easily not only with policies that devastated the wage class but with vicious prejudices against the members and culture of the wage class itself.

The Right's faith in the fairness of existing inequalities has more flexible roots, as shifts in intellectual fashion have sent the rhetoric of privilege careening all over a broad landscape of excuses. Back in the Middle Ages, the usual argument was that God had assigned each person his or her station in life, and asking questions about privilege was tantamount to questioning God's good intentions. The collapse of Christian faith in the eighteenth and nineteenth centuries sent the apologists of privilege scrambling for other options; theories of racial superiority and Social Darwinism put fake biology in place of religion. More recently, the insistence that modern industrial societies are meritocracies, where each person naturally gravitates to a place consistent with his or her abilities, fill the same dubious role.

None of these claims can be justified by the evidence. Track the individuals and families that populate the upper reaches of privilege in any modern industrial society, and you'll see something that resembles nothing so much as a pot of spaghetti sauce at a slow rolling boil. Individuals and families rise up from lower in the pot, linger on the upper surface for a longer or shorter period, and sink back into the depths. No one formula explains the churning; for every person who climbs into the upper ranks of privilege on the basis of talent, there's at least one who bullied and bluffed his way there and another who got there by sheer dumb luck—and there are many others just as talented who never succeed in climbing the social ladder at all.

The way down is a little more predictable than the way up, not least because it used to be a favorite theme for novelists. I'm thinking here especially of Thomas Mann's brilliant novel *Buddenbrooks,* which won him the Nobel Prize in literature in 1929. It follows a wealthy German family from the zenith of privilege through decline and extinction over the course of the nineteenth century. One of the reminders it offers us is that a life of privilege doesn't foster the habits that conduce to the preservation of privilege. Within a few generations, the descendants of the talented, the blustering, and the just plain lucky who clawed their way to the top become clueless and cosseted, unable to deal with the ordinary hurly-burly of life outside their bubble of privilege, and when something disrupts that bubble, down they go.

In ordinary times, as the spaghetti-sauce metaphor suggests, the turnover in the privileged classes is relatively steady and goes on without causing any particular disruption to the pot as a whole. To extend the metaphor, though, there are times when history turns up the heat suddenly under the sauce, a great bubble of steam rises to the surface, and the entire upper surface of the sauce is replaced in a single convulsive blorp. When that happens with spaghetti sauce, the result is usually quite a mess, and the same is just as true of the social phenomenon.

Here a different novel by Thomas Mann is a useful guide—the most famous of his later works, *The Magic Mountain*. What it's about, if I may sum up an extraordinarily multilayered tale far too crudely, is the world of European privilege in the years just before the First World War. There were plenty of novels written about that theme in the 1920s, when the memory of that vanished era was still fresh enough to be painful, but Mann went about telling his story in a typically unorthodox way. The slice of prewar life he chose, half metaphor and half microcosm, was a tuberculosis sanitarium in the Swiss Alps.

A bit of medical history may be useful here. Back before the development of effective treatments, tuberculosis was a death sentence for the poor. Those who didn't have to work for a living, though, could seek a cure in sanitariums in mountainous regions, where the clear dry air might give their immune systems enough of an edge to overcome the infection. There, with nothing to distract them but conversation and romance, the patients go round the narrow circles of their well-ordered lives, their every need taken care of by swarms of servants. Far below the magic mountain, on the crowded plains of Europe, things were happening and pressures were building toward an explosion, but the feckless viewpoint character Hans Castorp and his fellow-patients—Lodovico Settembrini, Clavdia Chauchat, and the rest—drift aimlessly along until the explosion arrives, the trance shatters, and Castorp is flung down from the magic mountain onto the killing fields of the First World War.

It's a fine read and I recommend it to anyone who has the patience—not that common these days—to take in a long, thoughtful, and richly ironic novel. That said, Mann's tale also places the current state of affairs in the United States and the rest of the industrial world in mordant focus. History paid Mann an elegant compliment, because the Swiss town where the International Sanitarium Berghof was located in Mann's novel is famous today for a slightly different gathering of the coddled and cosseted rich. Yes, we're discussing Davos, where the self-proclaimed masters of the world gather every year to take in speeches by movers, shakers, and tame intellectuals, and issue oh-so-serious rehashes of whatever vacuous notions are in fashion among the overprivileged just then. Look at pictures of Davos gatherings, and I'm quite sure that you'll be able to spot Hans Castorp among the crowd, blinking owlishly at the camera.

Castorp's vague cluelessness, certainly, is much on display these days, and not merely at Davos. That cluelessness takes many forms, but the one that's relevant here is the way that people high up on America's social ladder understand their own privilege. By and large, as already noted, the affluent on the leftward end don't think they have any privilege at all, while their counterparts on the rightward end think that their privilege is a straightforward reflection of their own superior talent, intelligence, and so on.

This is the magic mountain of our era—a mountain of privilege whose inmates either have no idea that they're privileged, or have convinced themselves that they deserve whatever they have and that those who don't have the same things don't deserve them. Far below the magic mountain, in the rest of the world, things are happening and pressures are building toward an explosion, but most of those up there in the heights have never noticed. It has never occurred to most of them that there's anything unusual about their lives, much less that some sudden turn of events could fling them down from the magic mountain and into a chaotic future for which most of them have made no preparations at all. That turn of events has not yet happened, but it is unlikely to be long delayed.

The salary-class aristocracy of the recent past, after all, had the power and wealth it did because the United States maintained hegemony over most of the world. Our empire—oh, I know, it's impolite to use such terms, but let's please be real—our empire, as I was saying, gave the 5 percent of humanity that lived in the United States access to a quarter of the planet's natural resources and a third of its manufactured products, and of course those were by no means equally distributed among Americans. The way that old-money families and tech-stock godzillionaires alike by and large rallied around the opposition to the Trump administration shows that they know perfectly well which way the wind is blowing.

In the history of every empire, there comes a point when the costs of maintaining the empire exceeds the profits. The American empire got to that point quite some time ago, and the policies that drove the U.S. working class into destitution and misery can best be understood as attempts to keep the privileged classes comfortable by shoving the rising costs of empire onto everyone else. The end of free-trade arrangements, the retreat from foreign military commitments such as NATO, and the first steps toward a modus vivendi with Russia, North Korea, and other rival nations were necessary steps in the retreat from empire.

Those first steps may or may not be followed up voluntarily during the years immediately ahead, but they will be followed up. Once an empire stops paying its own costs, down it comes, and if the ruling elite of the empire doesn't have the common sense to retreat from its unsustainable commitments in a deliberate way, they can expect to have the empire wrenched from their hands one way or another. Those choices define the future we can expect in America. Off in the distance, past the inevitable convulsions to come, we may just be able to glimpse the first dim foreshadowings of post-imperial America, and with any luck, of a nation a little less riven by rigid class barriers and so a little more likely to deal with its many pressing problems.

Mind you, fifty years from now, there will doubtless still be people who reminisce fondly about the good old days when the United States could pretend to be the world's irreplaceable nation, when Barack Obama used drone strikes to vaporize wedding parties on the other side of the world, and the deplorables knew their place. That's the nature of outworn aristocracies. On a broader scale, it's the nature of historical change—especially when the deep patterns of the collective psyche surge into action, splinter the magic that keeps an intolerable status quo frozen in place, and leave the presumptions of a fading era shattered in their wake.

Notes

Seriously? This is the era of the internet. If you have doubts about the accuracy of any of the assertions I've made in this book, go to your favorite search engine and look it up for yourself. Then go to a search engine you don't like to use, and do the same thing there—and notice the difference between what the two engines fetch you. That way you can arrive at an informed opinion for yourself, which is worth a great deal more than believing what someone says just because you read it in a book.

You're welcome.

Bibliography

Adler, Margot. *Drawing Down the Moon.* Boston: Beacon Press, 1979.

Allen, Jonathan, and Amie Parnes. *Shattered: Inside Hillary Clinton's Doomed Campaign.* New York: Crown, 2017.

Augustine of Hippo. *The City of God.* Translated by Henry Bettenson. Harmondsworth, UK: Penguin, 1972.

Ballard, Arthur C. *Mythology of Southern Puget Sound.* Seattle: University of Washington Press, 1929.

Berne, Eric. *Games People Play: The Psychology of Human Relationships.* New York: Grove Press, 1964.

Booth, Michael. *The Almost Nearly Perfect People: Behind the Myth of the Scandinavian Utopia.* New York: Picador, 2015.

Byrne, Rhonda. *The Secret.* New York: Atria Books, 2006.

Carroll, Peter. *Liber Null and Psychonaut.* York Beach, Maine: Weiser, 1978.

Chambers, Robert W. *The King in Yellow.* London: Wordsworth Editions, 2010.

Couliano, Ioan. *Eros and Magic in the Renaissance.* Chicago: University of Chicago Press, 1984.

Deloria, Vine, Jr. *God Is Red: A Native View of Religion.* New York: Penguin, 1973.

Dijkstra, Bram. *Idols of Perversity.* Oxford: Oxford University Press, 1986.

Ehrenreich, Barbara. *Bright-Sided: How the Relentless Promotion of Positive Thinking Has Undermined America.* New York: Henry Holt, 2009.

Evola, Julius. *Revolt Against the Modern World.* Translated by Guido Stucco. Rochester, Vt.: Inner Traditions, 1995.

———. *Ride the Tiger.* Translated by Joscelyn Godwin and Charlotte Fontana. Rochester, Vt.: Inner Traditions, 2003.

Fortune, Dion. *An Introduction to Ritual Magic.* Edited by Gareth Knight. Loughborough, UK: Thoth, 1997.

———. *The Magical Battle of Britain.* Edited by Gareth Knight. Bradford on Avon, UK: Golden Gates, 1993.

Goodrick-Clarke, Nicholas. *The Occult Roots of Nazism.* New York: University of New York Press, 1992.

Greer, John Michael. *After Progress: Reason and Religion at the End of the Industrial Age.* Gabriola Island, B.C: New Society, 2015.

———. *The Weird of Hali: Innsmouth.* Portland, Ore.: Arcane Wisdom, 2016.

Hawthorne, Nathaniel. *The Blithedale Romance.* New York: Norton, 1978.

Hughes, Michael M. *Magic for the Resistance.* Woodbury, Minn.: Llewellyn, 2018.

Jeffers, Robinson. *The Selected Poetry of Robinson Jeffers.* Edited by Tim Hunt. Stanford, Cal.: Stanford University Press, 2001.

Jung, C. G. *The Archetypes and the Collective Unconscious.* Translated by R. F. C. Hull. Princeton, N.J.: Princeton University Press, 1968.

———. *Synchronicity: An Acausal Connecting Principle.* Translated by R. F. C. Hull. Princeton, N.J.: Princeton University Press, 1960.

———. "Wotan." In *Civilization in Transition,* translated by R. F. C. Hull, 371–99. Princeton, N.J.: Princeton University Press, 1964.

Kübler-Ross, Elisabeth. *On Death and Dying.* London: Routledge, 1969.

Lachman, Gary. *Dark Star Rising: Magic and Power in the Age of Trump.* New York: TarcherPerigee, 2018.

Lévi, Eliphas. *Doctrine and Ritual of High Magic.* Translated by John Michael Greer and Mark Mikituk. New York: TarcherPerigee, 2017.

Lorenz, Konrad. *King Solomon's Ring.* Translated by Marjorie Kerr Wilson. London: Methuen, 1961.

Lovecraft, H. P. "The Call of Cthulhu." In *Tales of the Cthulhu Mythos,* Vol. 1, edited by August Derleth. New York: Ballantine, 1969.

Mann, Thomas. *Buddenbrooks.* Translated by H. T. Lowe-Porter. New York: Vintage, 1924.

———. *The Magic Mountain.* Translated by H. T. Lowe-Porter. New York: Vintage, 1927.

Maugham, W. Somerset. *The Razor's Edge.* London: Penguin, 1963.

Moldbug, Mencius (Curtis Yarvin). *An Open Letter to Open-Minded Progressives.* N.p.: Unqualified Reservations, 2015.

Orlov, Dmitry. *Reinventing Collapse.* Gabriola Island, B.C: New Society, 2008.

Regardie, Israel. *The Golden Dawn.* Edited by John Michael Greer. Woodfield, Minn.: Llewellyn, 2015.

Ritchie, Jean. *The Dulcimer Book.* New York: Oak Publications, 1963.

Seton, Ernest Thompson. *The Buffalo Wind.* Santa Fe, N. Mex.: Seton Village Publishing, 1938.

Sharf, Robert H. "Is Mindfulness Buddhist? (and why it matters)." *Transcultural Psychiatry* 52, no. 4 (2015): 470–84.

Spengler, Oswald. *The Decline of the West.* Vol. 1, *Form and Actuality.* Translated by Charles Francis Atkinson. New York: Knopf, 1926.

———. *The Decline of the West.* Vol. 2, *Perspectives of World History.* Translated by Charles Francis Atkinson. New York: Knopf, 1928.

Starhawk. *The Spiral Dance.* San Francisco: Harper, 1979.

Teitelbaum, Benjamin R. *War For Eternity: Inside Bannon's Far-Right Circle of Global Power Brokers.* New York: William Morrow, 2020.

Tennyson, Alfred. "The Passing of Arthur." In *Idylls of the King.* Mineola, N.Y.: Dover, 2004.

Thomas, Edward Harper. *Chinook: A History and Dictionary.* Portland, Ore.: Binfords & Mort, 1935.

Wilhelm, Richard. *The I Ching or Book of Changes.* Translated by Cary Baynes. Princeton, N.J.: Princeton University Press, 1950.

Index

BOOKS OF RELATED INTEREST

Egregores
The Occult Entities That Watch Over Human Destiny
by Mark Stavish

Occulture
The Unseen Forces That Drive Culture Forward
by Carl Abrahamsson

Men Among the Ruins
Post-War Reflections of a Radical Traditionalist
by Julius Evola

The Return of Holy Russia
Apocalyptic History, Mystical Awakening, and
the Struggle for the Soul of the World
by Gary Lachman

Russian Black Magic
The Beliefs and Practices of Heretics and Blasphemers
by Natasha Helvin

John Dee and the Empire of Angels
Enochian Magick and the Occult Roots of the Modern World
by Jason Louv

The Mystery Traditions
Secret Symbols and Sacred Art
by James Wasserman

Aleister Crowley in America
Art, Espionage, and Sex Magick in the New World
by Tobias Churton

INNER TRADITIONS • BEAR & COMPANY
P.O. Box 388
Rochester, VT 05767
1-800-246-8648
www.InnerTraditions.com

Or contact your local bookseller